Tales from Teesdale, Grassholm and Greena:

My story and journey

Wendy Cleasby

First Published 2005

Hayloft Publishing Ltd, Kirkby Stephen, Cumbria, CA17 4DJ

Tel: (017683) 42300
Fax: (017683) 41568
E-mail: books@hayloft.org.uk
Website: www.hayloft.org.uk

© 2005 Wendy Cleasby

ISBN 1 904524 33 8

A catalogue record for this book is available from the British Library.

Apart from any fair dealing for the purposes of research or private study, or criticism or review, as permitted under the Copyright, Designs & Patents Act, 1988, this publication may only be reproduced, stored or transmitted, in any form or by any means, with the prior permission in writing of the publishers, or in the case of reprographic reproduction in accordance with the terms of the licenses issued by the Copyright Licensing Agency.

Produced, printed and bound in the UK.

Cover photograph, the author at Greena, Stainmore.
Back cover photograph, Bob and Wendy Cleasby.

I dedicate this book to my father William Alderson, born 8th July, 1927, who died 13th September, 2004, aged 77 years. He was not just a father, but a friend and inspiration. I'm extremely proud to be his daughter, and will love him forever.

A handful of old photographs

and cards

That didn't mean that

much to me.

But now they are

my treasured

memories.

John Watson
(born 1874)

JohnWatson
(born 1847)

Elizabeth Watson
née Alderson
(born 1844)

Lancelot Alderson m. (1677) Elizabeth (née Fawcett) both of Thringarth

Henry (b. 1690) m. Mary Walker (Thringarth in Lunedale)

William (b. 1716) m. (1751) Mary Sanders

Thomas (b. 1748) m. (1802) Elizabeth Wallace of Romaldkirk

Thomas (1813-1857) m. 1843 Jane Dixon (1818-1857) of Hury, Hunderthwaite

| George (1843-1931) Ivy Cottage Hamsterley | Mary (1852-1937) West Hamsterley | Joseph (1854-1883) Hartlepool | Jane (1847-1915) m.1 John Nixon Dodds Terrace m. 2 Mr. Alderson Byers Greeen | Thomas (1849-1931) coal miner m. Ellen Peart Newfield Co. Durham | Eliz. (1844-1924) 1870 m. John Watson (d.1903) Greena Farm |

Thomas William (1864-1928) Railway House Kirkby Stephen m. Hannah Parkin (- 1942)

John (1874-1966) m. Annie Brown emigrated Canada

Ann (1872-) m. Thomas William Alderson Windmore Green

Mary Eliz. (1896-1972) never married

Simon Alderson 1747 m. Mary Mitchell of Muker

James 1775 m. Catherine Calvert

Simon (b 1781) 1802 m. Margaret Smith, lived Rowantree

Ann (1822-) m. 1843 John Watson (b. 1821 Lunedale son of Joseph)

Elizabeth m. Joseph Watson born Lunedale

Jane Watson m. John Longstaff lived Kaber & Middleton in Teesdale

Joseph George (1879-1961) m. Mary Isabella Robson no children lived Roe Bank, Brough

Elsie m Thomas Robson

Louis Alderson

Harriet Atkinson

Jessie Cowin

Alice Smith

Pennistone Green, Stainmore (second m. Eleanor Cleasby née Carter)

Wilfred   Laurie   Violet   Gwendoline   Geoffrey
         (b. 1926)

George (1889-) m. Grace

Thomas William (1893-1968) m. Ursula

Caroline (1891-) m. Arthur Page

George Gordon Middlesbrough m Joan Turner

Thomas William (b. 1925-1998)

William (1927-2004) m. 1955 Nora Dunn (b. 1934)

George Lenoard dau. Margaret

Graham   Martin   Karen

Colin (b 1956) m. Pam

Barrie (b.1958) m. Diane

Wendy* (b. 1960) m. Thomas Robert Cleasby * (b 1952)

Claire   Philip

Michelle (b. 1989)

Wendy (née Alderson) Cleasby
Family Tree

*George Alderson (born 1889) at Kirkby Stephen
with his wife Grace nee Hays*

Contents page
    Poem
    Introduction 13
    The Genealogist 14
1 About myself in Middlesbrough 15
2 My work 20
3 My Depression – when I began my research 23
4 My treasured memories 29
5 Thomas William Alderson, my Great-Grandfather 35
6 A new life in Middlesbrough, 1904 42
7 Some clues that I had to work on 47
8 The search for descendants of the family of Newfield 54
9 Canada and my long-lost relatives 64
10 A stitch in time: on the trail of the sampler 69
11 The family gathering 70
12 Lancelot, 1639, lived at Brough West 77
13 Hammill of Middleton-in-Teesdale:
    The Hammills come into the family tree 82
14 Jane Alderson - tricky to follow 85
15 I became a Cleasby 86
16 The retired Chief Constable of Devon and Cornwall,
    CBE and QPM 93
17 Hannah Hauxwell 95
18 Eerie feelings at Stainmore 98
19 Phone call with Glennis – 4/10/2001 99
20 He was trying to scare us (the missing link) 100
21 Tuesday 6 November
    Finding out about Startforth and Bowes, Cleasbys and Johnsons:
    Where Esther Cleasby lived (1861) 102
22 Signing the Queen Mother's book of condolence at
    Bowes Museum, Barnard Castle, Sunday 7 April 2002 110
23 Returning to the present 113
    Poem 116
    Acknowledgements 117

List of Illustrations

	page
John, John and Elizabeth Watson	4
Wendy (née Alderson) Cleasby Family tree	5
George and Grace Alderson	6
The author	10
Map	11
Ceasby Family Tree	12
School cross country team	17
Workmates at home delivery service	21
Bob Cleasby	24
Thomas William Alderson	25
2 Forbes Avenue and 27 Ayresome Green Lane	28
Thomas William Alderson	30
The author's parents	31
Various family members	32
William Alderson at Croglin Castle and Roe Bank, Brough	33
The author at Railway House	34
Kirkby Stephen, 1900	36
Letter from ICI	38
Thomas and Ursula Alderson	40
The old wardrobe	41
Broadfell, Orton	43
Low Moor, Orton	44
Death card of Elizabeth Watson	46
High Force	49
Laurie Robson and family	51
Newfield, Co. Durham	53
High Row and Stonebank Terrace, Newfield	55
Ivy Cottage, Hamsterley	57
The author, aged 8	**59**
The author	**60**
Saddle Bow, Lunedale	**61**
The author's parents	**62**
The Watson family, Canada	65
John and Annie Watson, Point Lake Farm, Saskatchewan, 1914	67
George Leonard Alderson, Hannah née Parkin and Carrie Alderson	68
Oxenthwaite Farm, South Stainmore	71
Pennistone Green, North Stainmore	72

Cumpston House, North Stainmore	73
Rowantree and Blackmoorgate, North Stainmore	74
Windmore Green, North Stainmore	75
Muker	78
Alderson Family History Society, 2000	79
The author's dad and niece	80
The author and Maxine and Mr and Mrs Pinkney	83
Greena Farm	87
Windmore Green and Grey's Lodge, North Stainmore	88
Dummah Hill, North Stainmore	89
Grey's Lodge, North Stainmore	90
Grey's Lodge, North Stainmore	91
Hannah's home in Cotherstone	96
Private House, Egglestone Abbey	103
Sleightholme Farm and Bog House, Bowes	105
Market Place, Barnard Castle	106
Cleasby's Yard, Barnard Castle	107
Bowes Museum	111 and 112
Michelle	114
The author	115

Transporter Bridge across the Tees, built in 1911

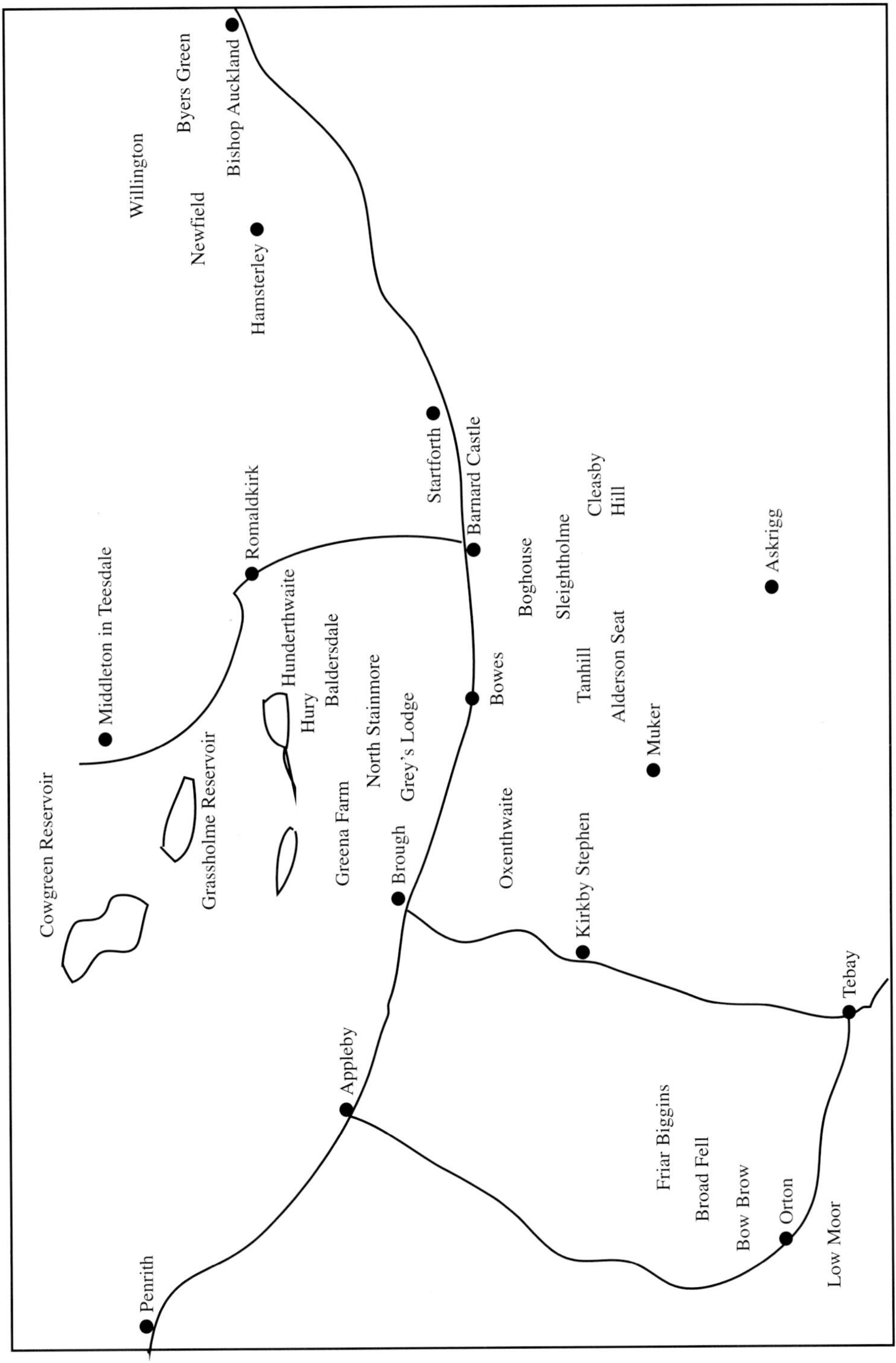
Bishop Auckland
Byers Green
Willington
Newfield
Hamsterley
Startforth
Barnard Castle
Romaldkirk
Middleton in Teesdale
Cleasby
Hill
Sleightholme
Boghouse
Askrigg
Hunderthwaite
Baldersdale
Hury
North Stainmore
Grey's Lodge
Bowes
Tanhill
Alderson Seat
Muker
Cowgreen Reservoir
Grassholme Reservoir
Greena Farm
Brough
Oxenthwaite
Kirkby Stephen
Tebay
Appleby
Friar Biggins
Broad Fell
Bow Brow
Orton
Low Moor
Penrith

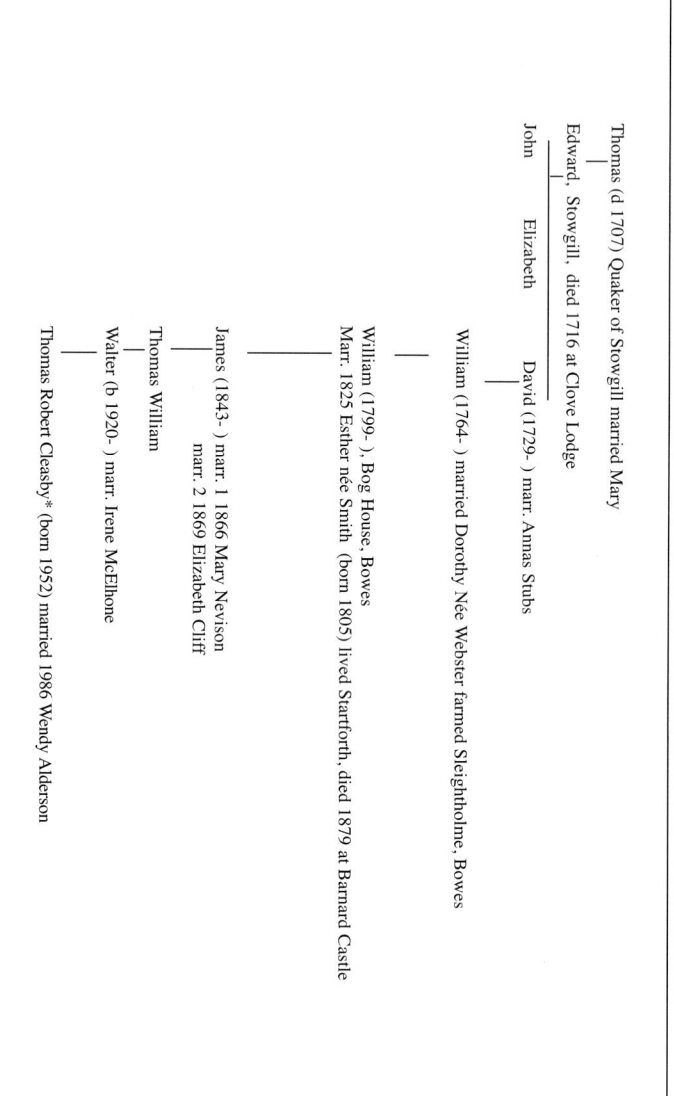

Cleasby Family Tree

Thomas (d 1707) Quaker of Stowgill married Mary

Edward, Stowgill, died 1716 at Clove Lodge

John — Elizabeth — David (1729-) marr. Annas Stubs

William (1764-) married Dorothy Née Webster farmed Sleightholme, Bowes

William (1799-), Bog House, Bowes
Marr. 1825 Esther née Smith (born 1805) lived Startforth, died 1879 at Barnard Castle

James (1843-) marr. 1 1866 Mary Nevison
marr. 2 1869 Elizabeth Cliff

Thomas William

Walter (b 1920-) marr. Irene McElhone

Thomas Robert Cleasby* (born 1952) married 1986 Wendy Alderson

Introduction

I have written this book to explain how, during a bad time in my life, I deeply needed to know more about myself and where I came from.

My journey puts lots of beautiful, tranquil places on the map, many old farm buildings stretching from Cumbria to Middlesbrough. It was an escape from the pain of the illness I was enduring. I wasn't with reality when I was on my journey. The countryside was away from everything that could hurt me.

My love of people in my family drove me to find out more about my ancestors' pasts. Everyone around me at this time was hurting me. No one was helping me. I was on my own. I escaped to dead people – the dead don't hurt. They would never hurt me if they were alive – my roots were with them.

I wanted to know what they did for employment and how they lived their lives. I discovered how communities grew up together, many families having ties for many generations, how farms were kept in the family for hundreds of years. I also learned how people moved from farming communities into towns to find work. I hope I have put some flesh on the bones of the people I never knew.

I hope this book opens a window to your soul to look through and find a way to achieve your aims and goals in life also.

The Genealogist

Wendy's spent most of her life trying to please,
That's Wendy – she works on Family Trees.

I don't mind, when I have the time,
I like astrology, her's is genealogy.
So we work out the equation
Then we start the investigation.

The knowledge it brings ties up the strings.
It takes you down paths where you've never been.
You end up knowing all things
About people you've never seen.

The work is fun, when you get a run,
On something that's hidden so deep.
To find such a small piece –
It can take all of your week.

The work is pressing
It becomes an obsession,
You're drawn into it far too deep.
Before you know, you're lacking sleep.

It's like a needle in a haystack.
You search every cranny and nook.
Sometimes if you're not careful
You'll find you're well and truly hooked.

But the pleasure this brings
It's like no other thing,
It puts flesh to the bones
Of those you've never known.

It's the paths that we take
That bring past times awake,
Genealogy is the key
That works inside me.

Chapter 1

About myself in Middlesbrough

I was an ordinary child living in a working class family and environment. I was sensitive, and I was very shy, but I always felt that I was an individual with a lot of will power, determination, and a strong spirit.

I got my looks from my grandma, but I thought I got my strong character from grandad. Grandad was physically strong – he was a stoker in the navy. My dad is meek and mild. I wanted to latch on to the strength of grandad, passed on to me by genes.

It wasn't easy being an only girl with two brothers. There was no one to confide in. My mother confided in me, through her illness, so I had to be strong – Wendy's duty is a religious thing. I never have been the kind of person who follows others like sheep, afraid to stand alone, or the kind of person who finds strength by leaning on others – Wendy is the helper rather than being helped.

I class this as a weakness. Through it, other people can try to mould you to be like them. I just want to be myself. If I want to do something I will try very hard to achieve it. I follow my instincts and listen to my inner self. I am inward-looking, but I won't be pushed out. In a way, I'm two people in one.

When I was nine years old, I was lucky or special enough to see a flying saucer.

It was one summer evening. In a bright blue sky, the saucer was a disc, shaped with lights shining out from windows around it. It was stationary for a while, and then it shot off so fast, much faster than an aeroplane or a helicopter. It was so clear in the sunlight. It just stopped in the sky. I stared at it. I was transfixed, rooted to the spot. When it shot away, I ran home as fast as I could. I think I was in shock.

My dad said, 'Write it down, and draw a picture!'

I did.

Both my father and my mother believed me, and still do to this day, as I was not a kid who would have lied. I told it as if it was Gospel truth. It was the truth.

This was in 1969, but I have not seen another since. Maybe I'm glad I have not. To have seen one once, as a child with a stable mind, was enough. If I saw one now, I wouldn't handle it so well. I'd be more frightened, if it happened now, after my illness. I'd feel that someone had picked me out to see it again – singled me out.

* * * * *

School years for me in Infants' and Junior Schools were happy days. But Secondary life was not. The school I wanted to go to was another. My two best friends, Susan and Gwen, stayed at Whinney Banks, but I had to go to Stainsby, where my brothers had gone before me.

I have good memories of the old days. My friend Susan Verrill, of Bruce Avenue, had a Japanese grandfather. She was very poor, but very clever, good at music and maths, and now an accountant. We would go carol singing at Christmas time, and once went collecting rags to take them to the Rag Shop over the border. We got lots of woollens, but only got paid sixpence - not much for all our hard work.

Gwen came from a family who owned their own home, Chalford Oaks in Acklam. Her dad had a car, and had a good job in one of the works, maybe ICI. Her mam's name was Sahra, and she was Gwen Sahra, after her mam.

Gwen was a lively, happy girl. She was a tomboy, as we would say in those days. She liked to run around and fight and have fun. She hated wearing skirts, and would never wear a dress. She loved to wear trousers. She wanted to be a boy, I think.

She was very generous, and would think nothing of sharing her pocket money if you were with her. I would go back to her house sometimes after school, and sometimes Susan Verrill would come with me, though Susan was not a tomboy, as Gwen and I were.

We would go over to the field to play football. I had a lot of energy, and was always running about. We would ride on Gwen's turquoise Hercules bicycle. She had just got it new for her birthday or Christmas, but you could have a go, or tan each other on it. She shared whatever she had. She went on a school trip to London, but my parents couldn't afford to let me go.

I think Gwen joined the Territorial Army. I've never seen her since my school days, and I wonder if she remembers me.

Susan, Gwen and I were parted once we reached Secondary School. My school was a lot further away than theirs. I used to pass Whinney Banks every day. I would always look around to see if I could see them, and sometimes I did. They looked happy with their school, but I was not happy with mine. I missed them so much.

I would look through the railings of Whinney Banks at lunch time when I passed. I would look to see if any of my friends were running around the athletics' track.

That was what I loved to do in the Junior School at Whinney Banks, running, especially cross-country. Running got rid of my frustration.

At school, I wasn't thinking about myself, but about my friends. I was worn out walking back and forth. It was a long way. I just could not let go of my friends – I would do anything for friends. Friendship was sacred.

But my friends had moved on. I thought they'd feel the way I did, but they could forget me tomorrow. I'm better on my own. I don't need friends. Friends hurt.

One of my favourite subjects at Secondary School was PE. I used to say that when I left school, I wanted to be a PE teacher, but I was told I would have to teach other subjects as well. I did not have a chance of that. I had messed up my schooling. I looked after Mam, and that was a big responsibility. I felt for her, but

(me)

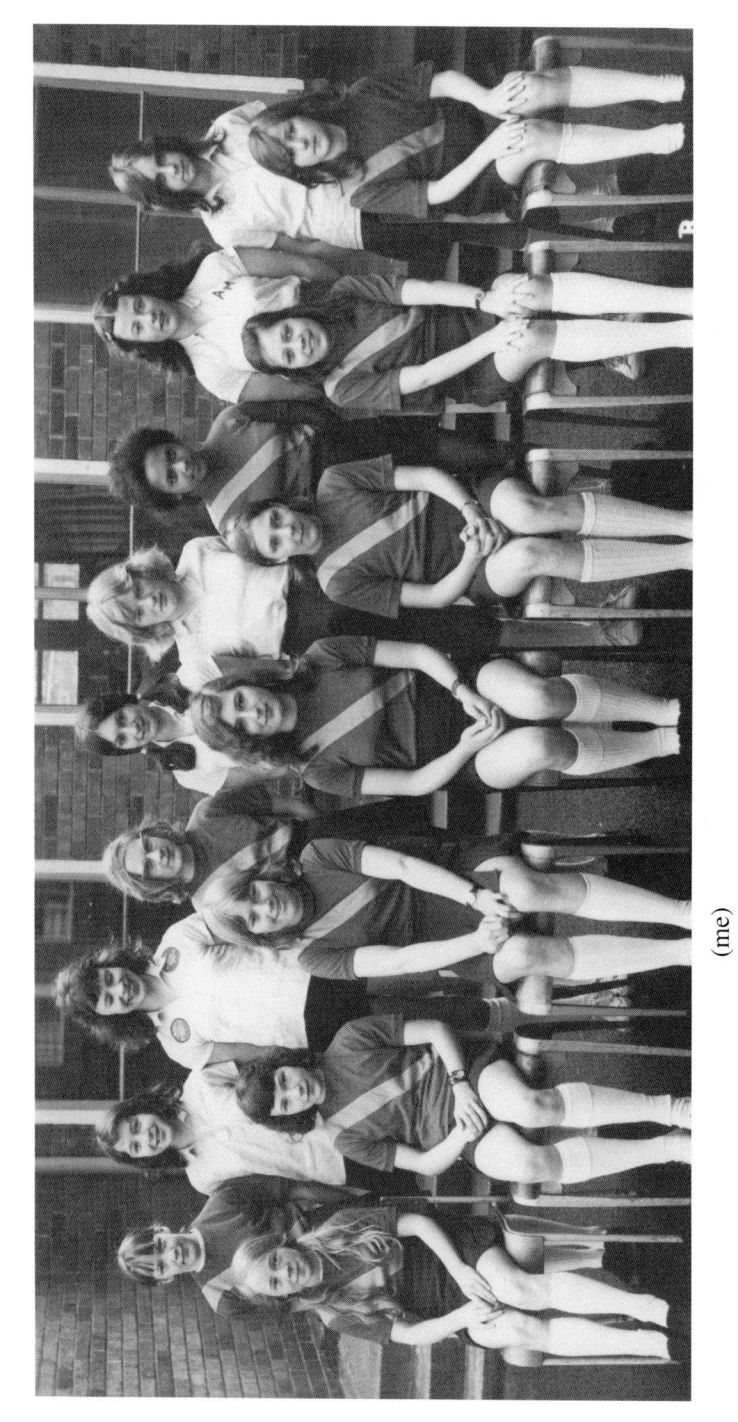

Cross Country Running Team at Stainsby school

she couldn't see that. She said she never made me look after her – it was me who wanted to do it.

When I was young, I only wanted to help Mam. I couldn't do enough for her. It was my love for her that made me want to help her. I was taught at church to help. Mam needed the help. I supported her.

At one time, I wanted to work in a church. I feel that I'm rather old-fashioned – maybe I should have been born in another century. That's how I eventually knew I was wrong at school – I felt opposite there to how I felt at church – I was calm and tranquil at church, and felt that I *belonged*.

I never really tried much at school. That was a big mistake, but I found that out later. No one at the time told me, but since, I've seen other people get on in jobs, and I've had to do cleaning, a job on brawn. I was fit. I was the right criterion for it. I think that when you clean, you don't have to learn. When you clean, you're like a machine – on automatic – like a robot. You're already programmed.

Friends had done typing and worked in offices, but my mother at the time didn't say that I might need something – perhaps my mother was too wrapped up in her own illness. That is why I am where I am now. My parents didn't explain I'd need the homework for later in life. Dad did a cleaning job. My parents didn't have anything that was ambitious. That is not a fault of theirs. Life just throws such situations at you. I realise now, that I am ambitious, though it was held back. I fight this, try to let my ambition come through.

I got into trouble at school. I had a strong character, and was rebellious – I hit people, and I didn't go to lessons. I think I became rebellious because of the responsibility I was putting on myself to help others. It was becoming too heavy a burden. The pressure had to come out somewhere. I didn't want to go to that school, didn't want Mam to be ill. I started periods, and I had no sister to talk to. I had been a hard taskmaster towards myself, but now, my life was going nowhere, and I hadn't been brought up to be this way.

Exams coming up in the third, fourth and fifth years put me right. I started taking notice.

I think I achieved seven CSEs by the time I left. I got history, physics – I remember the magnetism – English on the literature side, not grammar, and home economics. I can't remember the rest. I was very good at PE, but you didn't get a certificate for that.

* * * * *

When I left school, I took the first job that came along. My cousin, Jean, told me that there were new warehouses opening up in two months' time. I went around them, and asked for a job. It was a place owned by Littlewoods, and they said they would contact me.

Jean gave me some of her old clothes that she'd made herself – they were fashion clothes – Mam wanted me to stay a kid, but I wore those clothes, and wore them. There was a pink and white checked, A-line woollen skirt, and bottle green flared trousers with a button-fly – modern clothes, the like of which I had never had before! Fashion! At last!

On my seventeenth birthday a man came up the path to the house, where I was sitting on the step. He introduced himself as Mr Dave Griffiths, and asked me to go for an interview.

I didn't even know what an interview was, but I impressed them because I talked a lot. I got the job. Maybe my enthusiasm came through – my Auntie Heather said that I wouldn't take 'no' for an answer, and that was why I got the job.

I can remember helping Auntie Heather to move house in 1972, when the one in Ascot Avenue was being modernised. The house she was temporarily moving into was on the corner of Whinney Banks Road. How I loved to help people. I can remember running in and out of the removal van as fast as I could, carrying items carefully to help Auntie Heather do the job a lot quicker. Nobody likes the upheaval of moving home. She said I was a good help.

I was a very determined person. I thought I could do the job at Littlewoods even though it was hard work, man's work. I thought I was indestructible. I always pushed myself to the limits and beyond. But getting ill taught me to push no more. I was a human being who pushed myself too much. I later found that it was myself who hurt myself. I was my own worst enemy.

Chapter 2

My Work

I worked at Littlewoods for the next fourteen years.

I loved the job, and wanted to get the work done right. I was something of a perfectionist.

Mr Cowan was a great supervisor. He was fair and true. He was not afraid of helping out with work when needed – he gave something of himself, just as I did.

I was a general worker, which meant that I did anything, from sorting out parcels and postcodes to emptying wagons, cleaning and painting. I also filled the delivery vans with Liquid Petroleum Gas, known as LPG.

I made friends at Littlewoods, some of whom were true, and some not, though none were lasting. I was more for the work than the people though I did meet my future husband, Bob, at Littlewoods. He worked as a driver. I used to gas up his van for him.

Sometimes, in winter, the gas would leak out of the gun connector and freeze. I used to have to hit the screw on the fitting with a brick to release it, so that I could screw it off.

One day, I filled a van, as usual, and as the driver pulled away, he lit up a cigarette. To my horror, the van flashed and went boom!

The driver was taken out. He was shocked but okay. The pipe on the tank in his van had been fractured, and the gas had leaked out and caused the explosion.

That was it. I looked at the filling gun and thought, I'm not filling any more today – not if that happens. I continued filling vans after the day of the accident, but that day frightened me. I never really knew how dangerous the job could be.

I began to feel ill later, and believe that the gas could have had an effect on my nervous system. Some gas was released every time the tank in each van was full. It was a release or return valve. Some gas also was given out each time the gun was released and undone. I had to kneel down to floor level to unscrew the gun, and I've been led to believe that this particular gas falls to ground level. Could this have made me ill?

* * * * *

When Bob came to my house one day, and asked me if he could take me out, I said no at first, as I was very busy. I had a lot to do – decorating and gardening. I had my own house by then, with a mortgage, and my family lived with me. I had no time, I thought, to enjoy myself.

But then he asked me again, and I said that he could take me out, if he wanted, for my birthday, 15 October. It was 1984. I would have been twenty-four years old.

Wendy with workmates at Home Delivery Services

Wendy back row, with Denise and Susan

Wendy, Carol, Dave and Sheila.

He took me to the Yorkshire Dragoon at Maltby. I think it was a quiz night. We both talked a lot.

I discovered he was an only child with no mother. She had died when he was eight months old. He was in a music band. He was a bass guitar player. But most of all I discovered he needed to be loved. He had so much missed not having his mam, and brothers and sisters. I felt sorry for him.

I began to enjoy being with him, and he grew on me. I began to have feelings for him. But there were problems that went along with him.

He was set in his ways. The rest of his family wanted to keep him with them. They did not want to let him go. I lived with my parents and brother, and I knew that they would have to move if Bob and I got married.

When we began to get on together, some people at work began to treat us differently, not so nice. Maybe they were jealous. I really don't know. I think some people thought things were going too well for us, so they had to give us a hard time – interference and gossip from where no good could come, only harm. As two innocent people, we didn't seem to have the right to do as we wanted and make our own decisions.

The stress of it all did not help my health, and I began to get ill. I always had control, but I could feel it all draining away from me. I was going in on myself. I was not happy in my job any more. I had pushed myself hard all through my childhood, and I had worked hard, so I could have a better tomorrow.

When I had started Stainsby School, my dance partner had been a Thomas Yale. He became my first boyfriend. We met every Sunday to dance together at the Whinney Banks' Youth Club Junior Disco.

He was a lovely kind-hearted boy who sent me Valentine cards with beautiful verses in them. He came from a nice family, and I got on with them well.

He was more grown up than I was, even though we were the same age.

I liked him a lot, but I let him go, because I was not ready for a boyfriend. I was still a child, only eleven years old.

I'm sorry I let him down.

When I was older, I always thought about him, but it was too late – he had got married. I hope he's very happy.

With Bob, now I was grown up, it seemed that my life would start to get easy for me when I got married. When I told my mother I wanted to marry Bob, she was against it. She didn't want to lose me. I was a tower of strength to her. I had to tell her that I was going to marry Bob.

Thomas Robert Cleasby and I got married on 19 July 1986. I was twenty-five years old, and Bob was thirty-three.

But my life didn't get better with marriage – it seemed to get worse, and I was not strong enough to carry the extra trouble. I was already worn out.

Chapter 3

My depression – when I began my research

I was now married and I was really happy because I'd finally done something for myself – it felt like an escape.

We bought the house that we are still living in today in Acklam.

But I began to realize that something was wrong. I did not enjoy my work any more, the job I had once loved.

I had begun my research during my last few years of working at Littlewoods, after Auntie Dot Dunn died in 1981 or 1982, when I was about 21 years old.

Her death had a big impact on me, since I was very close to her. Dorothy Dunn was my mother's sister, and my Godmother, and we both had birthdays in October, both Libras. She didn't have much, but she was a nice person. When she was poorly, I visited her a lot in North Ormesby Hospital, and at home in Grove Hill. She had asthma, and smoked, which did not help. When she died, I felt a great loss, and I miss her to this day. She hadn't only been an auntie, but also a good friend.

She had given some old photos to Mam for safe keeping, and these got me going on my research. I did know where my heart was – in my research of my family's ancestors. This was what I was happy doing.

I became ill with depression. I continued working with the illness for two years at Littlewoods, but it finally took me – it won over me. I knew at last that it was time to take redundancy.

During my illness, my mind was always thinking of different things, as though it wasn't my own. I was trying to work out why I was in the mess I was in, but I couldn't get thoughts out of my head. That was torture. You need to be completely sedated on tablets to stop this, but then you can do nothing. I found the simplest things hard work. I was mentally worn out. I could not spell my name, it was that bad.

I have a strong will, and I tried to over-ride the effects of the tablets that were supposed to be making me better. I found it difficult to keep control of things, and that is very frightening. I was powerless as to how people were treating me. Some people wanted to see me go under. When I was a child, I had a lot of self-control, looking after my mother. It worried me that my illness meant that I couldn't be like this any more.

When I was ill, I was once in Darlington town centre when a gypsy came over to me to tell my fortune. She looked at my hand. I have a broken lifeline. It stops, but a new one starts half way across. She told me I had been ill but that I would get well. Had my life already been mapped out for me from the day I was born? Was I chosen to carry this weight? Was there a need for my existence?

Doctor Lewis knew what was wrong. He got me to talk and talk, as well as prescribing tablets. It took a lot of determination, but I worked very hard and rose

Bob Cleasby at the Newport Bridge, built in 1934

above the illness and found that there was a lot more to me than the person I was before it. I won in the end.

I was now a different character, with a different view on life. I was no longer headstrong, not after I had hit the floor. I knew I had left the old me behind – in the way I was, I'd been going down a wrong road that came to a dead end. I'd felt as though I'd had the whole world on my shoulders, looking after Mam – I'd thought I was indestructible and wouldn't crack, but I had. It had been killing me to be the way I was – I couldn't take the weight any longer. I couldn't be the perfect person – it was impossible.

My mother had been old-fashioned – girls helped in the house, and looked after the boys and men. I would be doing housework, and my brothers would just be sitting around, or I'd be doing the garden, and they'd be lying there, sunbathing.

Mam says this is the way I was, and at church, I'd been taught to help. From helping, I'd got the same feeling of satisfaction inside me that I'd got when I was in Church. My faith will go with me for the rest of my life, but by the time I started my periods when I was thirteen, I was beginning to realise that I hadn't had a childhood.

Thomas William Alderson, born 1893

By the time I was fifteen, I became anorexic, and my periods stopped – I didn't have a period for seven years, but I never told my mother about this.

I didn't want to grow up. I didn't want a boyfriend. I was trying to get small again.

With all the housework I'd been doing, I was whacked. I was too tired for school. Bob said that all this had held me back in my education.

When I was ill, I had spent much of my time shut up in my bedroom. I had run away from life and had lost the job that I'd loved, but I was safe in my home.

The first thing that I can remember hearing when I started to get better was the sound of the birds singing outside my bedroom window. It was like I had been born again. That old life had been dark and gloomy for such a long time, those dark days of despair. Even when the sun shone for others, it was not there for me. I was shut away where nobody else was. I was alone within my inner self.

I couldn't go forward, but I could go into the past. I found I could move in this direction. No one in this direction could stop me – because they were all dead.

It was at this time that I realized you could live your life somewhere else.

I think, to try to solve past mysteries, was an escape from my problems of the present. My nervous energies were channelled into this task. But I could only work on it when I was well enough. That's why it took me so long to do, but I always returned to it.

My grandfather used to say, 'What makes you bad also makes you better.'

Well, I think it's true, because if I worked too hard I became sick, but when I was well, I needed to do my work again. I was drawn to it. But what Grandfather had meant was the beer when he had drunk too much!

Grandad had liked his drink. He would spend all his money on it. Once, on ship, he had been told by the people in charge that he needed all his teeth out since they were rotten.

But the night before he saw the dentist, he spent all his money on drink, and had none left for the anaesthetic.

It was a case of having to have the teeth out, or he wouldn't be able to sail the following day. He had every bad tooth pulled out with pincers, without anaesthetic.

That would teach him not to drink. He always remembered it.

* * * * * *

As a child, I lived from being nine years old, at 2 Forbes Avenue.

I actually bought my own first home at 27 Ayresome Green Lane at the age of about eighteen. I took a mortgage on at a very young age, but I had the rest of my family move in with me. Mam and Dad helped me to do it. They paid me rent, and Dad was also guarantor for my mortgage.

I returned to photograph both houses in 2001. I was told that the house at Forbes Avenue was going to be pulled down. I'm glad I got the picture to keep even though the house had been left to ruin. The garden was well looked after when I lived there, as I took pride in it.

The other photograph shows the Ayresome Green Lane house much the same as when I lived in it.

*Wendy standing on the doorstep, 2 Forbes Avenue ready to be demolished.
I lived here from 1969 - 1975*

The house that I bought, 27 Ayresome Green Lane

Chapter 4

My Treasured Memories

I was born Wendy Alderson on 15 October 1960, at 3 Whitehouse Street, Newport, Middlesbrough.

My father is William (Bill) Alderson, born on 8 July 1927.

The house that Dad lived in until he was sixteen was in Linthorpe Village, which is now a part of Middlesbrough. The house, 427 Linthorpe Road, became Philips' Wool Shop, and now it is Keltz Restaurant, opposite to Stag Properties. Dad said that his parents, Thomas William and Ursula Alderson, used to rent out the front room on Election Day for the voting to the Conservatives, and then went next door, which was opened up for Labour voting. Dad used the old papers from the voting to scribble on.

My dad once had the last rites said as he was dying of pneumonia. Grandad got someone from the Salvation Army to do it. But the doctor opened his lung and got the fluid out. It was touch and go. If he hadn't pulled round, then I wouldn't be here today.

My mother, Nora Alderson, née Dunn, was born on 16 June 1934. The Dunn ancestors were from Eastgate Seamer, Scarborough, North Yorkshire, and my maternal grandmother's ancestors, the Kettlewells, were from Carthorpe near Bedale, North Yorkshire.

My father had one brother, Thomas (Tommy).

My grandfather was Thomas William Alderson. There were three generations of Thomas William, but five of Thomas.

My mam broke the mould, by choosing the names of Colin and Barrie for her sons, my two older brothers. She had to be different.

Maybe when you are different and don't follow suit, people give you a hard time. My mam always blames Tommy, my dad's brother, for making her ill in the first place. Mam became agoraphobic. Mam was Tommy's victim. He persecuted her because she took his brother away from him (Tommy never married) but Mam wanted Dad for herself to make her secure. Aunty Lily said that Tommy made Mam lose her confidence so much that she never got it back.

People are frightened of anything that is different. Many think that mentally ill people are dangerous, but most are not. They do most damage to themselves. Quite often, they hate themselves, for getting ill.

At the beginning of her illness, Mam became afraid of the way the world was. This began in 1962 with the Cuba Missile Crisis. It came on the news, and she went out, and everyone around her was laughing and talking as usual, as though nothing was happening. My Mam couldn't understand it.

You could say I was the victim daughter of a victim. Bob's family gave me a hard time, as Tommy had with my mam. Bob's father didn't want Bob to marry me, but to stay with him – Bob's mother had died when he was a baby. My mother wanted to marry my father for security. I wanted to marry Bob for stability – I wanted something to ground me.

And, like my mother, when I was ill in 1991, during the Gulf War, I couldn't get a perspective on it. I'd lost reality. I thought I was going to get bombed.

I have some of Mam in me, and I think the weakness in me comes through her. Mam says I was high and mighty, and that pride comes before a fall.

* * * * *

Grandad Thomas William Alderson lived at 29 Milton Street until he died on 5 November 1968. I was eight years old at the time.

I can still remember that night, Bonfire Night. We had let off many fireworks. I remember the Catherine wheel and sparklers, in particular.

It must have been around 7 or 8 p.m. when Uncle Tommy came round to tell Dad that our grandad had died.

Tommy had brought chocolate bars for us three kids, but these chocolate bars were still there on the side of the fireplace the next day. Nobody had eaten any.

When we kids heard the news, that was it, no more fireworks were let off. We loved our grandad. He was a pal to us, more than a grandad. We had always called him Dan, because when I was little, I called him Dandad. We had a song for him:

Dan, Dan, the mucky old man,
Washed his hair in a frying pan.
Combed his hair with the leg of a chair.
Scratched his beard with his big toe nail.

My grandad Thomas William Alderson

When we sang it, he was sure to laugh, but he would chase us around the house in mock-anger, since we were being a little cheeky.

Grandad always made a fuss of Bonfire Night. He was the one who bought us all our fireworks. He had the money. He was charge hand of the ammonia (dry ice) works at ICI, Billingham. He was always known as 'Hearty' at ICI because he got on well with everybody. Everyone liked him.

Grandad enjoyed the fireworks as much as we did. He did it all for my dad. He did a lot for my family. Grandad wanted to help, as I do. When he had the stroke he felt of no use. He wanted to die at the end. A strong man could not handle a life bedridden. He lived to help people.

It seems very hard that he died on 5 November, one of the days in the year when he meant so much to us, and on which he got the satisfaction of knowing he had helped us and made us happy. Bonfire Night was never the same again. Even now, I always think of him on Bonfire Night – even down to the chocolate bars left on the mantlepiece.

Life got hard after Grandad died. His help was missed. Before he got married, Dad got a pending sentence from defending Tommy in a milk bar – Tommy again, causing trouble – and Dad had trouble getting work after that. Dad had no job at all after he'd had his hernia operation. Mam and I had to go to Greenwood's, the pawnbroker in North Ormesby, to pawn her engagement ring and Dad's gold watch. I can still remember the door to the shop. It had a kind of a pulley system on the door to open it – there was a rope with a brick hanging on it, which went up when the door was opened, and down again as you shut the door from the inside.

Grandad had enriched us, but not only with money – there are still bits of Grandad in our hearts today.

Mam and Dad married 1955   *Mam and Dad*

Grandfather and his mother Hannah née Parkin

Thomas William Alderson, born 1864, Romaldkirk

George, grandfather's brother, lived at Bow Street, Middlesborough

Corrie, grandfather's sister

My Dad, William Alderson at Kirkby Stephen

The house at Roe Bank, Brough where my grandfather's uncle, Joseph George Watson lived in 1960

Wendy outside the Railway House at Kirkby Stephen, feeling rather ill

Chapter 5

Thomas William Alderson, my great-grandfather

Thomas William Alderson, my great-grandfather, was born in 1864 at Teesdale. He married Hannah Elizabeth Parkin at the Parish Church, Kirkby Stephen, on 27 November 1886. They lived in the Railway House at the side of the old railway line at Kirkby Stephen, where Thomas worked as a railway drayman, moving the coal from the trains.

The 1891 census records Hannah Elizabeth Parkins' parents, James, the head of the family, who was 52, and his wife, Mary, who was 50. It also shows James, their son, who was sixteen and worked on the railway line.

Hannah Elizabeth's family had a coal business in Kirkby Stephen. It seems likely that this is how my great-grandfather, Thomas William, met Hannah, by hauling coal destined for her family.

My great-grandparents' children were all born at Kirkby Stephen, my grandfather on 11 May 1893.

I think they came to Middlesbrough in about 1904, when my great-grandfather got a job as a drayman at Middlesbrough Station. He had a choice between Middlesbrough and Saltburn stations, and chose Middlesbrough because it was bigger. When they moved, they brought all their furniture by rail. People did, in those days.

Later, he worked at Middlesbrough Docks as a rolleyman, unloading cargo from ships.

From 1904 to 1905, the family lived at 67 Haddon Street, and from 1906 on, they lived at 77 Pelham Street.

* * * * * *

My grandad, son of Thomas William and Hannah Elizabeth, and also named Thomas William after his father, worked at Warrenby Iron Works for a short time and then joined the Merchant Navy, choosing to do the maximum twenty years. This was from 1914 to 1934. He was known by his workmates then as Nutty Alderson, or Best Pal. When the war came along, since he was already in the Navy for the full twenty years, he had no choice about being in it, and served with the Royal Navy for its duration. In 1914, 17 March, he is listed as being a stoker at HMS Royal Naval Barracks, Portsmouth.

During the war, he seemed to be sent to all the cold places. He was in Russia, and Siberia, where he'd seen the wolves running in the forest along the side of the docks.

His wartime experience gave him good references to go into ICI later, when he worked in the cold with dry ice. When he applied for the job, he already had the necessary knowledge about boilers – how the temperature gauge had to be watched.

Kirkby Stephen

Group photo taken about 1900. My grandfather, Thomas William Alderson born 1893 is fourth from the left on the front row. The boy sitting up next to him is his brother George.

Grandad had been friendly with the chief engineer, his future father-in-law, who taught him all he knew – Dad said he was a very clever man. Grandad was the iron man who never felt the cold.

In 1958, he left ICI after thirty years' service. By this time, Mr Falconer, the director, could write of him as almost a fixture of the institution. He received a gold watch, which Dad still has, with details of his retirement inscribed on the back.

In the wartime, he was shipwrecked twice. At one time, he was one of only two survivors, he and the chief engineer – he was said to have kept the chief engineer alive.

Grandad should also have been on the list of crew for the *Good Hope*, but for some reason, his name was missed off. This was the flagship, a Royal Navy armoured cruiser, which took a direct hit by the German fleet.

All hands went down, except my Grandad. His mates were gone forever. He felt guilty. He felt he should really have been dead with them.

He was on the *HMS Drake*, which, when carrying explosives for Geneva, was torpedoed in September 1917. I have an old postcard, a picture of him and his mates that he sent home to his family. It says that he wanted to get home to Pelham Street, and meet them all in the Empire Pub, which was just opposite.

He was also on *HMS Vernon* and *HMS Myrtle*. He received three medals for his wartime services.

I think my grandfather was very lucky. I'm proud that he survived each time that he could have been killed. It was as though he had been singled out to survive, which I think was a good thing, because he was so strong.

Grandad, and his father before him, were certainly stronger-minded than I am. Grandad was happy-go-lucky – I'm not – I'm a thinker. He was hardly a man who would get mentally ill – he wouldn't know what a nerve was.

I think of depression as a bowing down under pressure – a weakness. I feel that if I'd had the strength of my forefathers, I wouldn't have got depressed.

* * * * * *

My grandad, Thomas William Alderson (born 1893) married Ursula Crapper (born Kings Road, Linthorpe, Middlesbrough) at St Barnabas Church, Linthorpe. Her father, John Crapper, died at Richard Street, Jarrow in 1935. Grandad was thirty, and Ursula was twenty years old. Ursula was very beautiful. She had lovely hair and modelled hairstyles.

Grandad had a brother called George, and sisters, Caroline (Carrie), and Rhoda, who died when she was two years old at Kirkby Stephen, and another sister, Mary Elizabeth, known as Polly, who never married.

Polly was a normal child until she contracted polio when she was about thirteen years old. After that, she used to crawl around the floor when she was still young, and managed to drag herself around the room at home, but used a wheelchair to be taken outside, once Tommy, Dad's brother, came to live with her.

IMPERIAL CHEMICAL INDUSTRIES LIMITED
BILLINGHAM DIVISION

Telephone: Stockton-on-Tees 53601
Telegrams: Ammonia, Telex, Stockton-on-Tees
Telex: 58-523, Icibill Stocktn

BILLINGHAM
Co. DURHAM

Our ref. LJF/JES
Your ref.

28th July 1958.

Mr. T. W. Alderson,
29 Milton Street,
Middlesbrough.

Dear Mr. Alderson,

    It gives me very great pleasure to wish you a long and enjoyable retirement after your thirty years of faithful service to the Company.

    You had become almost an institution as the iron man who never felt the cold and we shall always remember your almost limitless energy as chargehand of the No.2 Urea Plant.

Yours sincerely,

(L. J. Faulkner)
Ammonia Works Manager

I.C.I./1625/01/B 1.57 KP

* * * * * *

The old wardrobe that I acquired when my uncle Tommy died in 1998, may have come from Kirkby Stephen, as it is over a hundred years old, and Uncle Tommy lived in the home in Pelham Street that his parents had lived in.

When Tommy died, it was just left there to be thrown out.

Well, nobody was going to throw this in a skip.

I got my cousin to get it on his car roof. The house was getting emptied the next day. I was going to get it and look after it for the rest of my life.

The wardrobe is in good hands. I will pass it on to someone in the family who will take good care of it. I love it. It is part of our ancestors' past.

* * * * * *

The last train on the Stainmore line ran in 1962. But in January 2002, after forty years of being closed, the Kirkby Stephen East Station, and part of the East Station Line, opened to the public. This was due to the hard work of the volunteers of the Stainmore Railway Company.

In 1962, demonstrators, with old boneshaker bicycles to represent previous times, protested at the loss of the Stainmore line.

In honour of the 2002 opening, the re-enacting of the vintage cyclists' protest took place. One of the happy demonstrators was Bryan Cowan, who is Laurie Robson's cousin – Laurie Robson is a relative of mine who is particularly close. The cyclists looked really proud men, standing there with their cycles. What an achievement for the people of Kirkby Stephen. What determination they had to get back what they once had. What fight!

Thomas William Alderson, grandfather born 1893 at Kirkby Stephen

Grandmother, Ursula born 1904

The old wardrobe over 100 years old

Chapter 6

A New Life in Middlesbrough, 1904

I can just imagine the level of energy and excitement that the four Alderson children, George, Tom, Carrie and Polly, would have displayed during their first ever journey to unknown Middlesbrough.

They would have taken all their furniture and worldly goods on that journey, leaving behind them all their relatives, not to mention all of their school friends. They left behind also, their sister Rhoda, who had died at Kirkby Stephen.

Let's hope that Middlesbrough's town life matched their expectations, because the Kirkby Stephen area was a lovely place to leave.

The reason for the move was that their father, Thomas William, was offered a better job, with more money. Future job prospects for the children would also have been better in Middlesbrough.

I hope they were impressed with their first sight of Middlesbrough Railway Station, which was much bigger than the one from which they had left.

It was this uprooting from Westmorland that explains my being here in Middlesbrough today. Maybe one day I shall return to my roots. I do think that I would be more suited to a life in the countryside. When I am walking over the same ground that my ancestors would have walked, and seeing the views that they would have seen around the Greena Farm area, near Kirkby Stephen or Thringarth Village, my heart is happy, and I feel as though I belong.

Here, life is much more easy-going than in the town. There is all the open space, the lovely peace and calm, the fresh air and tranquillity, and the lovely people. Everybody I have ever met in the area has been helpful, caring, honest and kind, always having time to talk and to help me with my research, and giving me directions to derelict places that are not shown on today's maps.

If I had not begun my research, I would never have known any of this. Every time I got new information, I was on a high. It gave me a buzz and a feeling of control. Instead of my illness controlling me, I was controlling what I was doing. It was a strong feeling of fighting the blues, and winning.

* * * * * *

Thomas William Alderson, born in 1864 in Romaldkirk, my great-grandfather, was the illegitimate son of Elizabeth Alderson, who in 1857, was orphaned at the age of twelve.

In 1861, as shown on the census, Elizabeth was the sixteen-year-old live-in domestic servant for Mrs Ann Kipling, a widow aged 65 years, of Low Newhouses, Chapel of Ease, Wesleyan Chapel Buildings in Hury-in-Hunderthwaite. Elizabeth also taught Sunday School and Mrs Kipling owned and ran the church. Hury-in-Hunderthwaite was a few scattered houses and farms near Baldersdale.

Broadfell, Orton, in 1891 was the home of John Watson and Elizabeth Watson née Alderson

Low Moor, Orton

Elizabeth's illegitimate children, including my great-grandfather, were born after this time. I don't know the circumstances, but the father of the children was a miner from Durham way.

Elizabeth married John Watson in 1870. He was from a good family, and took her in with her children. She had two more children, Thomas William Alderson, born 1864 and Jane Dixon Alderson, born 1868 who died 1874 aged 5 years and 2 months. So it is possible that the father's name may have been Dixon. So I could be a Dixon?

The family moved to Orton in Westmorland, where Anne, John, Joseph, George and Jane Watson were born. They lived at Low Moor, Orton, and the 1891 census shows them living at Broadfell in Orton. Thomas William Alderson, Elizabeth's eldest son, married Hannah Parkin at Kirkby Stephen in 1886, during the time that his parents were at Orton.

John Watson worked on the railway. Eventually, he moved, with his family, from Orton to Greena Farm, North Stainmore.

John Watson's sister, Jane Longstaff, and her husband, John Longstaff, also lived at Orton in 1871. John Longstaff was a railway signalman. Four years later, they lived at Kaber near Kirkby Stephen, and then moved to Middleton-in-Teesdale. Their ten children were born at the three different places.

* * * * * *

Bob and I visited Orton. We had to drive up a very narrow lane to get a photograph of Broadfell Farm, where Elizabeth and John Watson had lived with their family. After travelling a few metres, the lane ahead was full of twenty or more young schoolchildren, led by their teachers. They instructed them to hang on to the wall stones, or climb on to the dry stone walls at the side of the lane so that our car could get through. They never expected to see a car in a lane that was so narrow and overgrown. The children were smiling at us. They thought it was great fun.

When we reached Broadfell, I asked the owner if I could take a photograph of the house. The lady was very nice, and said that I could. She showed me the stream, the fresh water supply used years ago, that ran at the side and the front of the house. The house would have been built close to a water supply to save carrying water for miles each day, and there was a supply at hand for their animals and cattle.

When John Watson lived here in 1891 with Elizabeth and the children, he would have had to travel to Tebay to work as a railway platelayer.

In Loving Memory

of

ELIZABETH,

WIDOW OF THE LATE JOHN WATSON,

Of Greena, North Stainmore,

Who died April 1st, 1924,

Aged 79 years.

The interment will take place at Brough Churchyard, on Friday, April 4th, 1924. Cortege leaving residence, North Road, Kirkby Stephen, at 1-0 p.m., for Service in Brough Primitive Methodist Church, at 2-30 p.m.

Sleep on dear mother, and take thy rest,
For God hath called when He thought best,
Our loss is great, but thine is gain ;
In Heaven we hope to meet again.

Death card sent to Middlesbrough of my great-great-grandmother, Elizabeth Watson née Alderson

Chapter 7

Some Clues That I Had to Work On

1. Grandfather saying to my mother:
    'Brave Lady, marrying into the family who was related to Mary Ann Cotton.'
2. I began my Alderson family tree with only a copy of the 1962 will of Mary Isabella Watson of Roebank, Brough, which mentioned a relative in Canada.
3. A death card of Joseph George Watson, husband of Mary Isabella of Roebank, Brough. I have a photograph of the house.
4. A death card of Thomas William Alderson of Brough.
5. A photograph of my grandfather at school in Kirkby Stephen around 1900.
6. A death card of Rhoda Alderson, daughter of Thomas and Hannah Alderson, who died and was buried at Kirkby Stephen aged two years and three months.
7. A death card of Elizabeth Watson of Greena Farm.
8. Mam, Dad and Grandad visited Kirkby Stephen and the Croglin Castle Hotel in the late 1950s.

* * * * * *

What I also had was a lot of motivation, a strong will, and plenty of drive to find out what was unknown to me. It became my mission to see what I could find out. Nothing was going to stop me. It was all systems go.

Bob and I went to Kirkby Stephen, and went in the exact same pub where Grandad had taken Mam and Dad when they were courting in the 1950s. It wasn't until later that I found I had followed in Grandad's footsteps, generations on. I had thought I was going through everything alone, but were the souls from the past around me, helping me?

I began to put the pieces together. At this time I was about thirty years old. Grandfather Dan Alderson had died when I was eight years old. My father knew nothing more than the clues themselves, nor did his brother come up with much more at this time.

My father never asked questions about the past, but he said that our oldest living relative was his cousin George Leonard Alderson of Beechwood. This was in 1984.

He was the first relative I visited and interviewed, just as though I was a reporter. I loved it. It was really me. I wrote down every little detail he knew, and left no stone unturned.

What I really wanted to make was something from nothing, just like putting together a jigsaw puzzle, but without the picture on the box to copy.

When I interview a family member, I feel great love for them. I look for character, expressions, similarities to other family members, present and past. My love for them, and meetings with them, are warm to the heart and soul. It is such a truly rewarding experience for me, one that I feel I was born to.

Bob drove me everywhere, since I can't drive. Bob made it possible for me to follow my next move each time.

* * * * * *

George Leonard Alderson from Beechwood was a handsome man, tall and slim. With his elegant stature, he would stand out in a crowd. He told Bob, Dad and I that he had just married a woman called Lilo, who was from Brunswick, Germany, and that he was going to join her there.

He had been in the war against the Germans, and his tank had been hit twice, but George held no grudge against the German people, and had holidayed in Germany. I was glad to have met him before he left to be with Lilo.

He took us into his back garden. We had tea under a parasol. It was a glorious sunny summer's day.

George was pleased to see me take an interest in the past – he also liked family history. He gave me the original marriage certificate of Thomas William Alderson and Hannah Parkin, my great-grandparents. He knew a lot more than I did. The family came from Romaldkirk, County Durham. I had never heard of the place at this time.

Elizabeth Alderson's parents had died young from TB, and Elizabeth and her brothers and sisters were scattered around County Durham. George showed me a sampler on the wall in his hallway. It was made by Elizabeth Alderson of Romaldkirk in her tenth year, 1855. This would have been two years or so before her parents died. It was in a lovely glass frame, and was beautiful. It had survived all this time.

Now I had a little more information to work on.

* * * * * *

We went to Kirkby Stephen to see Norman Parkin, the son of James Parkin, and my grandad's cousin on his mother's side. He lived in a wood-built house, called Cushang, which was raised above the ground. He had been in the Navy most of his working life, and had brought keepsakes back with him from distant places, including ivory carved figures.

He said that Thomas William, my great-grandfather, was a strong man, could swim in waters with high currents, was a county councillor, and a well-known poacher.

Norman had a sister, Elsie Parkin, who had a café or coffee shop in Kirkby Stephen, but had died of cancer in the 1960s. He said his mother used to keep three guineas hidden behind the fireplace for a rainy day.

Wendy and family at High Force

Norman was something of an eccentric too. After his death, people we spoke to said he had lived alone and never bothered much with people, but that he'd liked his holidays abroad.

He had been away at sea for most of his youth before coming home and building his own house. The house was different, since it was all of wood and built on stilts. Steps led up to it. His parents used to have a coal business.

* * * * *

I put all my information together, and looked next at the copy of the 1962 will, that of Mary Isabella Watson. Mary Isabella was the wife of Joseph George Watson, the youngest half-brother of my great-grandfather, Thomas William Alderson. Names like 'Robson', 'Sowerby' and 'Wooff' were mentioned in the will, but my father didn't know them.

There was also in the will, the name Ursula Jenny Harvey of Kirkby Stephen.

I thought I would take a chance, and wrote to an Alderson of Kirkby Stephen, since my name was Alderson. I got the address from a telephone directory of the area.

She passed the letter on to another Alderson of The Crescent in Kirkby Stephen, who wrote back saying she was the eldest daughter of Louis Alderson. Louis was the son of Ann, the half-sister of Thomas William Alderson, my great-grandfather.

The letter was also passed on to Ursula Jenny Harvey, so it eventually found its way to the person named in the will. Ursula Harvey turned out to be one of Laurie's relatives, coming also from the Louis Alderson side of the family.

Ursula wrote back to me saying that although her name was on the will that I had mentioned in my letter, she did not know of my grandfather, who was also named in the will. Ursula asked around, and then took the letter to her niece, Pam Chilton, whose father was Leonard Robson, another relative of Laurie, and whose name had also been on the will. Now I had found a Robson.

Pam wrote, telling me about Laurie Robson, who perhaps could help me. Then a letter arrived from Mr Laurie Robson who was born in 1926. It was wonderful. Neither Laurie, my father nor myself had known about each other.

Mr Robson said he was also related to Elizabeth Watson of Greena. Elizabeth Watson, formerly Elizabeth Alderson of Romaldkirk, was my father's great-grandmother who lived at Greena Farm. Bingo! I had found them!

Laurie and I wrote three or four letters back and forth – he was as excited as I was, and glad that I had gone to so much trouble to find him. I had never been so excited in all my life. My hard work had paid off.

In the letters, Laurie confirmed the names of his half brothers and sisters that had been on the will. These were the Sowerbys and Wooffs. He said he did not know who I was. I told him I was the granddaughter of Thomas William Alderson,

Visiting Laurie Robson at Penrith with the clock from Greena Farm

Laurie Robson, Wendy Cleasby née Alderson, William Alderson and Michelle Alderson in the front

whose name had also been on the will.

He told me that he and his brothers had been coffin bearers for Mary Isabella Watson. Laurie and his descendants were from Windmore Green, North Stainmore, near Greena Farm.

He had just retired from farming and had bought a bungalow in Penrith.

Bob and I visited Laurie when we went to Lake Ullswater, and took Dad with us. We often go to Pooley Bridge, which is not far from Penrith. We had our niece with us also, and were on our way for a camping holiday. Laurie was a strong man, but looked nothing like my father. I would never have met him if I had not traced my family. I think my ancestors would have been proud. I asked him if he knew anything about Newfield or Canada, places mentioned in the will, but he knew nothing.

He pointed to the clock in his living room, telling me that he had just got it mended, and that the clock had been originally from Greena Farm. I just stared at it with amazement – the actual clock that Elizabeth Watson née Alderson had at Greena was in Laurie's house, staring me in the face.

It was a wonderful find. I was over the moon. I would never have seen it, if I hadn't made this happen myself.

Laurie also had a notebook listed with births, deaths and marriages of Watsons and Aldersons, as well as a record of grain, crops and so on.

Laurie's friend was with him. He kept giving my niece popcorn. She was looking very bored. She just wanted to get to the lakes to go camping. The very young are not interested in family history – what they want is fun. As usual, I was trying to please everyone, my niece, Laurie, and the people of the past.

After this visit, I knew I had to work on Greena Farm, and find out about the Canada and Newfield mysteries. One thing had led to another – I began the search due to my interest and desire to know, and things had almost got a momentum of their own. I was enjoying myself.

* * * * *

One Bank Holiday, my husband Bob and I, Dad, my brother Barrie, and my niece, Michelle Dawn Alderson, went to Newfield, County Durham, for the first time. We asked around, the people in the street, and those in the local pub, but could find nobody by the name Alderson.

I decided we should search the cemetery. The others were a little unsure. They weren't really interested themselves, and although they did want to help me find what I was looking for, they couldn't really understand what was driving me so hard. They looked on with amazement, puzzled and a little frightened at what I was doing – my determination. But I was looking for some hidden clue as to why I had been so ill with depression.

I needed to find out where I came from. Ancestors help me. I knew I was joined to them. I was a person trapped in a shell. I looked at the graves not knowing which side of life I was on.

We found one large black marble tombstone bearing the name of Thomas Alderson of Newfield, born 1849, husband of Eleanor née Peart. Thomas died in 1937, aged 87 years.

Yes, I had found what I was looking for, one of the brothers of my great-great-grandmother, Elizabeth Alderson of Romaldkirk. My hard work had paid off again, but now I had to work on Thomas only from the details on the headstone.

Me at the grave of my great-great-grandmother's brother Thomas born 1849. He died in 1937 in Newfield, Co. Durham

Chapter 8

The search for the descendants of the family of Newfield

First, I got census returns for Newfield, County Durham. Census returns are attainable from the reference library or the archives. The returns gave me addresses. I wrote to 15 High Row, Newfield, since this was where my relatives had lived, but the man who lived there had lived all his life in the house, and what I was interested in was before his time.

    I bought birth, death and marriage certificates from the registrar's office at Bishop Auckland, County Durham, to get information and addresses. I knew from looking at my own birth and marriage certificates that you could get a lot of information from these about other members of the family.

    I found that Thomas, born in Romaldkirk in 1849, had gone to live in Newfield with his auntie and uncle of the name of Dixon, when both his parents had died from TB in 1857. Mrs Dixon's maiden name was Alderson. She was my great-great-grandmother's auntie and Thomas's mother was a Dixon before marriage, so there is a double connection between the Aldersons and the Dixons.

    Thomas's parents, Thomas Alderson and Jane née Dixon, died at Hunderthwaite. Thomas had been a stonemason and innkeeper at Hury in Hunderthwaite. The death certificate of Jane (née Dixon) showed that she died on 16 August, the widow of Thomas Alderson.

    The Dixons were miners at the local pit. From the census return from 1871, I found that Thomas, at the age of 21, was a miner at Newfield, County Durham, and later became a mine deputy.

    Perhaps if his father had lived, Thomas would have followed him in the trade of stonemason, though by the time his parents died, they had been running an inn. Thomas married Ellen Peart and had a family in Newfield.

* * * * * *

I put an article in the local Newfield newspaper appealing for further knowledge of the family. If nobody answered, the trail would stop. I hoped that someone out there remembered something about them.

    Then one day the telephone rang. It was a Mrs Morton from Dorset. She said that she was the daughter of one of the sons of Thomas of Newfield.

    It was very exciting for both of us to be speaking to each other, and to this day, we still write often. Maureen told me what she knew about the family. Thomas of Newfield's son, also Thomas, was a lay-preacher at the Primitive Methodist Chapel, Newfield. In 1900, the family home was 4 Stonebank Terrace, Newfield.

    It was a cherished memory of Maureen's that her grandad Joseph Alderson had a half guinea on a watch chain. The glass on the fob was cracked – it was supposed to have been trapped in the door of Stephenson's Rocket on its inaugural

15 High Row, Newfield

14 Stonebank Terrace, Newfield

run. The watch and fob had been the possession of his father, Thomas Alderson, who is reputed to have had links with George Stephenson.

Maureen told me that her father, Norman Alderson, born in 1927, had died in 1997, so I never got to meet him.

It turned out, though, that my uncle Tommy had known Norman Alderson, and had even gone to visit him in Bishop Auckland during the 1970s, riding there on his bike. Tommy came up with this information about three months before he died in 1998. He had never mentioned any of it before.

He said that when he had lived with his Auntie Polly, she had written to various people, and Tommy had posted the letters. He remembered names, like 'Robson', and 'Annie Robb' who had lived in a little pit village in County Durham. His auntie Polly had also written in the 1950s or 1960s to a relative called Cummings. He could remember the names, but not any addresses.

When I asked why he'd never mentioned this earlier, he said he didn't think anybody would be interested! But I was! If only I had asked him, it would have made my research easier, and I might have got to visit Norman before his death. What a loss! Although, I did find his daughter instead of him.

* * * * * *

I later found from census returns that relatives of George Stephenson had lived at Newfield, County Durham. Both the Stephensons and the Dixons lived at Low Row, Newfield, and both heads of the families were miners.

George Stephenson was said to have taken care of his relatives when he had done well for himself.

Finding details on the census returns confirmed that there was a connection between the two families. George Stephenson also picked a John Dixon to be his assistant with his projects.

* * * * * *

What became of the other brothers and sisters of Elizabeth and Thomas Alderson when their parents died of TB in 1857? I again put articles in the newspapers of Newfield, but there were no answers. I decided to look up deaths in St Catherine's House Registers, which are on microfilm in the reference library at Middlesbrough.

Over the course of my research, I have looked in these registers many times. You need to know what you are looking for before you consult them. You might look something up, but if you don't get a lead, you might not get anywhere for the next six months or so.

Then you may get a letter, and that will start you off again with new information. This kind of research is the type that you can't rush, but it comes naturally when pieces of information start to come together.

In this way, I searched for many years, and found that during the time that

Ivy Cottage, Hamsterley was the home of George and Mary Alderson in 1930

Elizabeth Alderson had been working as a domestic servant for Ann Kipling at Hury-in-Hunderthwaite, her sister Jane, and brother, Joseph, lived with their aunt and uncle, William and Mary Alderson. This was in 1861, according to the census returns for Hunderthwaite.

George and Mary, another brother and sister of Elizabeth and Thomas, lived long lives, but neither married. They had died in Ivy Cottage, Hamsterley Village, which is not far from Newfield.

In 1851, as can be seen from census returns, their parents, Thomas Alderson and Jane (née Dixon), had been living with their family in Christopher Bank, Romaldkirk, and Thomas's brother, John Alderson, and his wife, Mary, had been living with them.

The father of this Thomas, also a Thomas Alderson, born in 1768, died on 30 December 1839. He was a farmer and mason, and died of pleurisy, in Hunderthwaite, his daughter, Jane, being present at his death.

* * * * * *

We visited Ivy Cottage. The man that lived there let us look around inside, and take a photo of it. The man said it used to have a little lean-to room on the side that could have been a shop. The owner had in his possession the deeds for as far back as the house went. Mary was on the deeds in 1909. She had bought the house from a Joseph Ralph Robson, who was a grocer.

Neither George nor Mary married or had children. When they died, Ivy Cottage was left to the youngest child of their sister, Jane Alderson. This was Mary Elizabeth Cummings née Alderson, who had married Herbert Cummings. Another child of Jane was Jane Annie Robb née Alderson. At one time, Mary and Annie lived near Newton Aycliffe. These are the families that Polly Alderson of 77 Pelham Street, Middlesbrough, wrote to.

I had traced all the family now, back to the source, Jane Alderson, born in 1847 in Romaldkirk, sister of my great-great-grandmother, Elizabeth Alderson, born in 1844.

* * * * * *

I always knew that, in 1857, my great-great-grandmother's parents, Thomas and Jane née Dixon died of TB at the Inn at Hury where they lived.

I had obtained an old map of 1856, Hunderthwaite, from Northallerton Archives, and it showed an inn named the Half Moon Inn.

We found our way, and asked a Mr Alderson of Howgill Grange, Hury, if he knew anything about it. He told us that the inn seemed to be the same place that became the Hare and Hounds Inn. It must have changed names. The water supply was from Molly's Well. This Hare and Hounds Inn is now West Hury Farm Cottages.

We paid a visit, and the owner has in his possession an article from a

Wendy aged 8 years

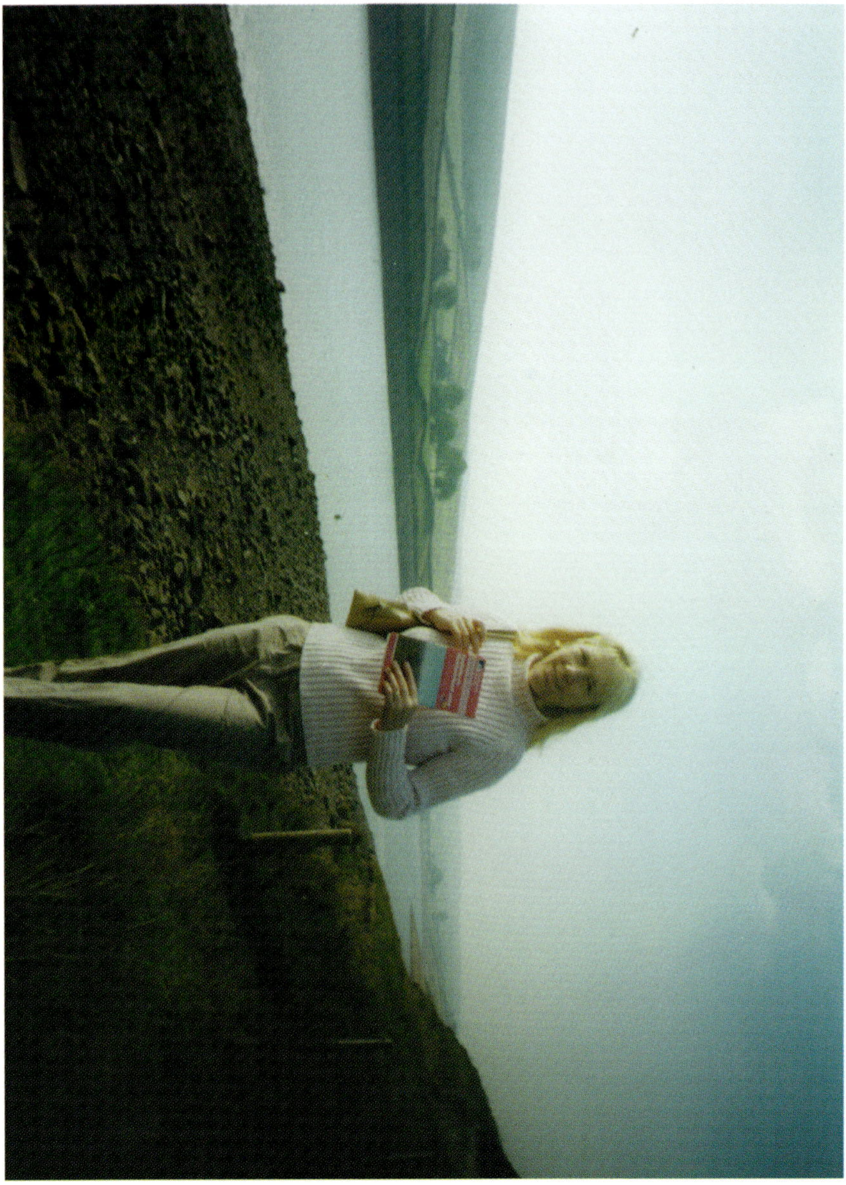

Saddle Bow in Lunedale

Dad and mam at Whitby, 16th June 2004, mam's 70th Birthday

newspaper of 1863 about Mr William Alderson of the Hare and Hounds, Hury in Baldersdale, retiring from farming, and selling his farm, stock, crop etc.

This William took over the inn when my family died in 1856. William was my Thomas Alderson's brother. It was probably at this time that the inn changed names, from the Half Moon Inn in 1856, to the Hare and Hounds in 1863.

Nobody living there ever knew that it had once been called the Half Moon Inn, not even the locals who had lived there all their lives. So they had learned something new too, their local knowledge to pass on to other folk.

Chapter 9

Canada and my Long-Lost Relatives

A person named on the will, John Watson, was still puzzling both me, and Laurie Robson from Penrith. The will only said 'John Watson, Canada'. We did not have a clue who he was.

I wrote to district probate, asking them to send me a full copy of the will, which turned out to be different from the one we had. The new copy had on it an address in Canada from 1962, 10434-147 Edmonton, Alberta, Canada.

I wrote to the National Archives of Canada in May 2000, explaining that the people at the Canadian address of 1962 were my relatives. I received a letter back from the archives in Canada on 31 August 2000. A search of Edmonton City directories had come up with the fact of a removal in 1970. My relatives had moved to 9415 151st, Edmonton.

I wrote to the new address, saying that they could be my long-lost relatives. I also rang the lady who lived there. She could not believe that I had rung all the way from England.

The lady I spoke to was Glenna, the wife of the John Watson on the will, who was my great-grandfather's half brother. Sadly, he had died. Glenna gave me the address of her granddaughter, a Christine Hennes of Saskatchewan. Christine had been trying to do a family tree, but had little information to go on.

Christine said she was really pleased to hear from me. She said she hadn't known that there were any relatives in England. She had not known that her great-grandfather had brothers and sisters here.

Her research had revealed that John Watson and Annie Brown had married, and that Annie had given birth to a son, also named John, in Sunderland. The family had emigrated in 1911. They went from Liverpool on April 28 to Montreal in Quebec, which they reached on 10 May. The ship was called Lake Champlain, and it was a converted cattle boat. They went by train from Montreal to Toronto. Annie Brown's mother and brothers had already emigrated.

I knew nothing of all this before this time, and the relatives in Canada had not known of us. If only my great-grandfather was alive now, I'm sure he would be pleased at the way I had bridged the gap.

Getting in touch with the Canadian relatives gave me a wonderful feeling. These people from Canada belonged to me. I was alive - somebody, real. Every person I found was bringing me back from my depression to the real world, making me stronger, enriched.

Christine Hennes and I became good friends, and she hopes we shall meet, and that she will be able to visit the old homes of our ancestors. We have passed to each other lots of information and photographs, and I was especially pleased with the one of the house built by John Watson and Annie at Point Lake Farm. There is a resemblance in John Watson to my father and me. Christine can also see the

Watson family in Canada

Rebecca  *Justin*

likeness. Christine is a teacher in Canada. Her husband is called Brian, and they have two children, Justin and Rebecca. They hope one day to meet my niece, Michelle.

My later research found that John Watson's cousin, William Longstaff, emigrated in 1911 from Middleton-in-Teesdale to Tofield in Canada. He was born on 12 December 1879 at Kaber. William had often written back to his family, saying how good it was out there, and that there was plenty of land. William's parents were John Longstaff, born 1846, and Jane Longstaff, née Watson, born 1849.

On the 1861 census Jane Watson is living with her father, John Watson, born 1821 at High Dowgill. Next to him at Low Dowgill, shown on the census returns of Stainmore, is the family of Thomas Raine. The next family shown are the Johnsons of Littlethwaite, Stainmore.

I find that I seem to be connected to Stainmore by the Aldersons and the Watsons, and also by my marriage to a Cleasby. The Cleasbys are also connected to the Johnsons and the same families in Stainmore. The 1891 census shows the ancestors of my relative and friend, Laurie Robson, as living at Gill Bank, Stainmore, next to the Watsons and the Raines.

* * * * *

John Watson and Annie Brown moved from Toronto to Yonker, Saskatchewan, in 1914. They settled beside the lake, and called their farm after it – Point Lake Farm.

With much research, I found that Annie was born in 1869. Her parents were married on 15 July 1867 at St Cuthbert's, Gateshead. Matthew's father is shown as being William Brown. Jane Stephenson's father was Thomas Stephenson, a miner from Wreckington. I am sure this Stephenson family and the Stephenson connection with my Aldersons from Newfield, are relatives of George Stephenson, who invented Stephenson's Rocket in 1829.

John Watson, Annie and son, Point Lake Farm, Saskatchewan, Canada, 1914

George Leonard Alderson born 1911. Living in Germany in 1994. Died in 1995

George Leonard Alderson with grandmother Hannah née Parkin

George Leonard Alderson with his mother Carrie

Chapter 10

A stitch in time: on the trail of the sampler

The will of Mrs Elizabeth Watson (formerly Alderson), who died at Greena Farm in 1924, states that her sampler was left to her grandson, George Alderson.

It must have been passed to his nephew, George Leonard Alderson of Beechwood, for me to see it hanging in his hallway when I visited him at the start of my research, in 1984. We visited him again a few weeks later. The sampler was no longer on the wall, but parcelled in brown paper. He had said he was going to give me the sampler.

George told my dad that he and Lilo were going to live in Germany in Lilo's house. He said he was now giving the sampler to his daughter, Margaret. We said nothing. That was the last we saw of him, and we thought that Margaret must have got the sampler.

In March 2001, I put an article in the *Evening Gazette*, trying to trace his daughter, Margaret Alderson, to see if she had the sampler, and to find out particularly for my dad, when his cousin, George Alderson, and Margaret's father, had died. The lady who had lived next to her father at Beechwood saw the article and phoned me with Margaret's address. I wrote to Margaret, but she said she did not have the sampler, nor any contact with Germany.

I wrote to the German Embassy in order to trace George and Lilo. I got a letter back, written in German, which I did not understand. A friend, Brian Davidson, took it to a person he knew who read German. The letter gave the address, and I traced the telephone number.

At last, I got in touch with Lilo Alderson, who told me that George had died on 12th September, 1995.

He had lived a lot longer than we thought. The funny thing was that my father, Bill Alderson, had been in Germany in July 1995, and if he'd had the address, he might have visited him.

Lilo said that she did not have the sampler. She said that most of his things had been left behind. What a chase, and what a disappointment. Had the sampler been left in a brown paper parcel for the bin men to take away? I would rather it was hanging on the wall in some antique shop. Surely such a lovely item would not have been thrown away?

How I wanted to find it and show it to the Canadians. I feel sad that Elizabeth Watson had been let down. It would have been a family keepsake, needle-crafted in 1855 in Elizabeth's tenth year. I would have given anything to own it, or even to see it again. I would even have gone to Germany to get it. Maybe, I just hope, that somebody has misplaced it, or forgotten that they have it.

Nobody searched for the sampler like I did. I managed to save the old wardrobe from Kirkby Stephen. Maybe one day, I may find the sampler or anything else to go with it. God willing, I would take good care of them.

Chapter 11

The Family Gathering

It was Wilfred Robson's funeral. Wilf was Laurie Robson's brother. Laurie is a very nice man and always has time for people. We get on really well, maybe because our birthdays are two days apart. At times, I would ring Laurie a lot, as he would help me find places on Stainmore, since he had lived his life there. He knows all the names of the little farm houses dotted about. I told Laurie, from my findings, that his Robsons were from Oxenthwaite. This triggered his memory of his mother taking him as a child to see an old bent-over man at Oxenthwaite.

Laurie had been really close to Wilf, his eldest brother, who had been a shepherd for most of his life at a farm in West Brisco. This farm had been owned by an Alderson family for many generations. At the funeral, I met Geoffrey Robson, Laurie's younger brother, and his wife, Wendy. We shook hands. She spoke of the family tree. I told her I loved mysteries, and detective work. Geoffrey and Wendy said they did too. I shook hands with old Mr Wearmouth, who had been living with Wilf before he died, and also with Laurie's daughter. This was the first time we had met.

* * * * * *

Laurie had lived in Cumpston House, and at Pennistone Green, North Stainmore. Blackmoorgate, where Tom and Diana Moore live today, is on the road edge opposite Greena. In 1900, a James Sowerby lived at Blackmoorgate. All the neighbours in those days were very close to each other, and most families in an area would be related. But over a hundred years ago, the Methodist prayers were taken from Blackmoorgate. It was a meeting place.

Windmore Green was the home of Laurie Robson's great-grandfather, born in 1874, and totally blinded due to an accident in the mine. He became a grocer. His first wife was Ann Watson, who was my great-great-grandmother's daughter. When Ann died, he married again, his second wife being Jane Brown.

Laurie said that Rowantree house, which is close to Windmore Green, was the one the Watsons lived in with the Alderson relatives. Margaret Alderson, née Smith, also lived there. She is a relative of one of my husband's family members, Esther Cleasby, née Smith, who lived nearby at Grey's Lodge. It really is a small world.

* * * * * *

I took photographs of Grey's Lodge on the evening of 25 April 2002. This was the first time we had visited the place. The year before it had been out of bounds due to foot and mouth.

Oxenthwaite Farm, South Stainmore

Pennistone Green, North Stainmore was the home of the Robsons in 1900. It is now holiday cottages.

Laurie lived at Cumpston House, North Stainmore

Rowantree, North Stainmore

Blackmoorgate, Stainmore

Windmore Green, North Stainmore

It was a lovely feeling to eventually walk right up to it, and get inside. Bob and I were really pleased to have found it, since it has been derelict for about a hundred years, and is not listed on any maps. Both my husband's and Laurie's ancestors had lived there.

We had to go through two gates and up a public walkway to reach it. There were wild rabbits running around everywhere. With so much untouched nature, it was beyond belief. The wind was howling at us. We sheltered inside, where it was so calm. It felt just like the home it would have been hundreds of years ago to our ancestors. From the doorway of the house, the view from the top of the hill was magnificent.

* * * * * * *

Laurie found this address in an old notebook of his Mam's:
Mr & Mrs, J Alderson, South Barnaby, British Columbia, Canada.

We think this address is that of the uncle of Laurie Robson's mother, Elsie Alderson, from Windmore End, but the people are all dead, so we can't ask them.

* * * * * * *

Tracing back from what I knew of Greena Farm, I found that a descendant of Laurie's mother's family was Simon Alderson, born on 1 June 1851, son of William Alderson and Jane Dent.

Researching back from before the death, on 1 April 1924, of my great-great-grandmother, Elizabeth Watson, I found that Simon Alderson and Priscilla Hall were married in 1894, and that they had lived at Greena Farm in 1895, when their first child was born. This Simon must have moved away because he died in March 1924, aged 72 years, at Lamplugh Mill.

I think that when they moved away, Elizabeth née Alderson and John Watson moved into Greena. John Watson's mother was Ann Alderson, who was the sister of Simon. John Watson, born 1847, and Simon Alderson, born 1851, were therefore cousins.

Chapter 12

Lancelot, 1639, Lived at Brough West

One day, I received a phone call from a member of the Alderson Family History Society, asking if I wanted to become a member. They had seen my articles in the newspapers, where I had tried to trace Alderson relatives.

At first, I said that no, I didn't want to join. I was happy working on my own, doing my own thing. My work was personal. About six months later, I received another call. They said that if I could submit to them seven generations, they could join me up with others. It crossed my mind that I would be parting with my hard work, but I thought it sounded as though it would be worth it.

My descendants go back to a Lancelot Alderson of Brough, who bought some land at Thringarth. The land was for the remainder of a thousand years. The land was called Ibank in Thringarth, Lunedale, Romaldkirk. Lancelot sold the land in 1659 to Michael Rayne. Loans in this area were paid back to Lady Bowes, an ancestor of the late Queen Mother. Lancelot had sold the lease of the land to a Michael Rayne. At the time, these two lived at Thringarth. It's lovely to find out these things that you would never have known.

I met the Society members in September 2000, and 2001, at Muker Public Hall. The members were all very nice and friendly.

Most of the land of our ancestors is now underneath the Grassholme Reservoir in Lunedale. They say that when the valley was flooded to make the reservoir, the farm houses were left underneath. If there was ever a drought you might be able to see the walls still standing, if you looked down from a height.

The land Ibank on the photograph is in front of the triangular shaped fields. The land has been cut away to make the valley bigger and deeper.

* * * * * *

On Wednesday October 1st 2003 I visited Grassholme Reservoir with husband Bob. I looked in the vistitors' centre for the first time, which has a map of the area. It shows Thringarth Pastures, which was not on our map. We now know exactly where Crooked Acre Farm, Ibank, and Thringarth Pastures were, places where my ancestors once lived.

We walked along the shoreline as the water was very low, because of the lack of rain in the summer months. I said to Bob, 'Isn't it lovely to be walking on the spot where my ancestors farmed and lived?'

I felt I belonged there. I felt at home. I asked Bob to pick a piece of the stone that had fallen down from Ibank to take home as a keepsake. I asked him to pick a piece that would stand out. The piece he picked up and gave to me was heart-shaped.

My heart belonged in this place. It was given to me by the man I love.

Middlesbrough to Muker with travel sickness. Wendy at Muker, it was a terrible trek for me

Alderson Family History Society Muker, September 2000. Wendy front row kneeling down

My dad and niece Michelle at Romaldkirk

This journey that had brought me here, begun due to my illness, Bob had travelled too. He had been through the ups and downs with me. We had travelled this journey together until we had come out at the other end.

We still had enough love to keep us together, even though it had been a very hard journey that would have broken weaker people for sure. We could have become very bitter and broken but we had battled through together to find calmness and peace. We had stayed strong. We had weathered the storm. We had passed the test, and come out good.

Chapter 13

Hammill of Middleton-in-Teesdale:
The Hammills come into the family tree

John Watson's Canadian cousin, William Longstaff, born in 1879 at Kaber, died on 27 January 1953. The addresses of contact at the time were for his next of kin, his sister and his brother, Mary A. Hammill of Barnard Castle, and Francis Longstaff of Darlington.

William had sent home to Mary a quilt he had won. It was of all the states or provinces in Canada. He paid 50 cents to win it. He also sent Mary a guinea every Christmas. Mary had a shop, and Laurie can remember going there with his mother.

I got in touch with Mrs Vera Pinkey, whose maiden name was Longstaff. Her husband was from Saddlebow in Thringarth. She put me in touch with her daughter, Maxine Payne, who was also interested in family history. She told me about the Longstaff of Middleton, whose wife was Jane née Watson. That rang a bell – not only did I find that Jane was a Watson, but also that she was sister-in-law to my great-great-grandmother, Elizabeth née Alderson, who married John Watson.

One of the elder brothers of William Longstaff who emigrated to Canada, was Thomas Longstaff, born 7 April 1871. He married Emily, and had two children. Maxine told me that they had a taxi business in Middlesbrough, but that was all she knew.

I checked burial records and found the deaths of Thomas Longstaff, 1947, Emily, 1938, and their daughter, Florence Ruston Longstaff, who also died in 1947.

I then looked at electoral registers, and found addresses for them, including the son, John T. Longstaff:

    1930   286 Linthorpe Road and Zetland Place, Middlesbrough
    1935   the same
    1938   Zetland Place and 10 Park Vale Road, Middlesbrough
    1947   94 Stockton Road, Middlesbrough
    1949   the same

In the Trades Directory of 1930, I found the address of the taxi firm:
Thomas Longstaff & Son, Taxi Cab Proprietors, 286 Linthorpe Road and Zetland Place, Middlesbrough.

I placed an article in the *Evening Gazette* to try to trace them, but had no luck. The only person to ring me was a Mr Dent, who said his father had the Dent's Garage in Middlesbrough in the 1930s, next door to Longstaff's Taxis. He said they had a taxi each, father and son, and used to take people from the station down Linthorpe Road.

Mr Dent's parents were Fred Charles Dent and Elizabeth Dent. The two families worked next to each other for twenty years. Mr Dent, the one who rang me,

Wendy and Maxine, Middleton-in-Teesdale

Mr and Mrs Pinkney

used to clean the taxis out, when he was a young child. They have Dent's Garage in Middlesbrough today.

My trail on the Longstaffs stops. I don't know what happened after 1949 when John T. Longstaff lived at 94 Stockton Road. He, the remaining son, was not buried in Middlesbrough, like the rest of his family. I wonder where he went?

But with further research on the Longstaff families, using census returns in the Stainmore, Brough, area, I found:

    1881   Kaber Buildings – a John Longstaff, born 1846, and Jane Longstaff, née Watson, born 1849.

    1881   High Green Cottage, Warcop – Robert Longstaff was born at Warcop.

    1891   Croft House and Rose Cottage, Warcop – a John, Thomas and Matthew Longstaff.

    1851   Robert Longstaff and Elizabeth Alderson, servant, Brough High Street.

All of these are likely to be related to each other.

Chapter 14

Jane Alderson was tricky to follow

I always thought that Jane Alderson, sister of Elizabeth Watson, née Alderson, never married, since she seemed always an Alderson. Only after many years of trying to find her death certificate, which was difficult, because I did not have the details, did I find the truth.

Jane, born 1847 in Romaldkirk, had two children out of wedlock, so they were called Alderson. She then married John Nixon, and had a child, Jane Ann Nixon, but John died a few years later. Jane married again, this time to George Alderson, so Jane became an Alderson again. She then had a child, Mary Elizabeth Alderson, who married Herbert Cummings.

I never thought she would go back to being an Alderson after being a Nixon – in looking for details, you expect that a woman's last name may change with marriage, but not that it would be the same, or go back to being the same as it was previously.

This reminds me of an old rhyme that my mother often says:
Change the name, and not the letter,
Marry for worse, and not for better.

It was the youngest child of Jane Alderson, Mary Elizabeth Cummings, who had inherited Ivy Cottage, Hamsterley, from her Auntie Mary Alderson. There were no shares with the other children.

Jane's second husband, George Alderson, was a widower when he married her. His wife had been Ann Raw of Arkengarthdale, and after she died, he married Jane, who brought up her own children, and George's to his first marriage.

Whatever happened to Jane Alderson's stepsons? I found out that the father of Ann Raw was Jonas Raw, a miner. John William Alderson, Jane's first stepson, was born in 1860, and married Frances Jane Tuck in Bishop Aukland on 5 June 1880. Thomas Alderson, the second stepson, was born, probably, in 1866. There were also the older children of Jane Alderson, born out of wedlock – Thomas William and John Joseph Alderson. In 1891, the family lived at 63 Holly Houses, Woodland.

Jane Alderson died on 9 June 1915, aged 68 years, at Dodds Terrace, Byers Green. The son in attendance was recorded as John Alderson. I don't know if this was her stepson, John William Alderson, or her son born out of wedlock, John Joseph Alderson, since the middle name of the John Alderson on the death certificate was not recorded.

Chapter 15

I became a Cleasby

Laurie Robson once said that his grandmother on his father's side was a Cleasby. That was a coincidence, since I had never heard of the name before meeting my husband, Thomas Robert Cleasby. We didn't research this line until later.

My husband's great-grandfather was James Cleasby. He was born at Bowes. He died at the age of 28 years from a blast when a boiler exploded at an iron works in Thornaby.

James Cleasby's mother was Esther née Smith, and his father was William Cleasby. Esther and William lived at Dummah Hill around about 1925.

Esther Smith's parents were Thomas Smith, a grocer, and Jane née Atkinson, who from 1794 to about 1814, lived at Grey's Lodge, and later at Green Cragg. All of these places are a stone's throw from Greena Farm and Windmore Green, where Laurie's maternal ancestors and my ancestors lived.

In 1841 William Alderson lived with his first wife Elizabeth née Johnson, and then in 1843 with his second wife, Jane née Dent, at Grey's Lodge. Jane's father was George Dent, a collier from North Stainmore.

How funny that a distant relative married a Cleasby in Stainmore, and then so did I in Middlesbrough! I wonder if this was meant to be?

* * * * * *

On Thursday 25th April, 2002, after Bob finished work, I met him and we decided to get photographs of Dummah Hill and Grey's Lodge, North Stainmore. We spoke to a kind man at Blackmoorgate, who said that nobody had lived at Grey's Lodge for about a hundred years. The house is now derelict, but situated on the top of a hill in a lovely location, with the front of the house looking down on the beauty of unspoilt nature at its best. Wild rabbits ran around our feet, and then back into their warrens to safety.

We also found out that Greena Farm, the last home of my great-great-grandfather, had new owners since the year before.

Our year's new car is running fine, but I'm still not the best of travellers on these winding hilly roads of North Stainmore.

* * * * * *

In September, 2003 I visited Greena with Bob. The new owners are the Willcocks, and the lady is an artist. She welcomed us in to have a look around after I told her that my great-great-grandmother, Elizabeth Watson, née Alderson, had died at Greena in 1924. It was beautiful. The walls were painted white over the plaster. There was a stone-slab floor downstairs, and upstairs, very wide wooden floorboards. The house

Wendy and Marian, the new owner of Greena in 2003

Windmore Green, North Stainmore

Grey's Lodge, North Stainmore

Dummah Hill, North Stainmore

Grey's Lodge, North Stainmore

Grey's Lodge, North Stainmore

had the original stone stairs and wooden beamed roof, the original windows and doors, all smartened up. It felt like home.

What a very special day, the first time I'd been inside Greena. I had seen every single room. What a wonderful experience. It was like going back in time.

I told the lady I would love to buy it if I was ever rich, but she said she would never sell. She loved the house too.

* * * * * *

Laurie's paternal grandmother was Eleanor Cleasby née Carter. When her husband, Joseph Cleasby, died, she married Tom Robson, Laurie's grandfather. Both families lived at Pennistone Green, Stainmore.

Joseph Cleasby, Eleanor's first husband, was born on 13 October 1845, at Heggerscale, Kaber. His parents were Robert Cleasby and Nancy Cleasby, formerly Longhorn. They were married on 3 January 1839, in the parish church of Kirkby Stephen. Nancy's father was Shamas Longhorn.

In 1797, there was a marriage at Muker between Anthony Cleasby and Alice Alderson. In 1805, a daughter, Alice Cleasby, was born. She later married a Mr Dent, who lived at Hury.

Hury is where my Alderson ancestors, Thomas and Jane née Dixon, also lived, innkeepers, who both died in 1857, leaving six children orphans, all under the age of 14 years.

I also obtained information that a Mr Cleasby, whose family was from Kirkby Stephen, became the Dean of Chester. When he died, he left to the National Trust, a settle, a clock, and a crib to be kept and shown in the Crosskeys pub at Cautley near Sedbergh in Cumbria.

Chapter 16

The retired Chief Constable of Devon and Cornwall, CBE and QPM

Laurie told me a long time ago that it was said there was a connection in the family with a retired chief constable. He thought that it was a cousin of his mother, Elsie Robson née Alderson.

But how could I contact him? He was a big nut to crack. I felt I would never get his address, but I had to get a letter through to him. I had his name, so I phoned the police station, and confirmed that he had retired. I told the secretary that I wanted to get in touch with him since he could be a relative.

The name I had was 'John Alderson', and I had heard his name on the television. But the Alderson I wanted had been a rather distant relative of Laurie's mother, and I couldn't be sure if this Alderson was the man I was looking for. The secretary couldn't give me his address, so I asked if I wrote a letter to her, with a letter to him inside, would she pass it on? She said that she would. Brilliant.

I couldn't believe my luck when he actually wrote back to me. In his letter, he sounded genuine, and interested in what I was doing. He told me his father was from Leyburn, and that he was a member of the Alderson Family History Society, number 13 or 33 – he wasn't sure himself which. This was the society that had contacted me.

On 1 July 2001, I had a conversation over the telephone with the Chief Constable. I explained who I was, and why I had traced him. I told him it was very kind of him to write back to me, as he did not know me.

He said I sounded a nice Yorkshire lass, and had, he could sense, an ambience about me, and deep religious ways, with love for those who have lived before us, a natural willingness to find out about them, and trace the families, joining back up again the connections that had been lost, like the missing links of a chain.

It certainly seemed as though the Chief Constable had time for me. Really, it had been a case of me wanting to be connected to someone who had done well at investigations. This was what I was doing now, investigations. He was a success in this.

I asked if he would be going to the meeting of the AFHS at Barnard Castle. He said it was a long way for him to go, but he would have loved to, as his father, Ernest, went to Barnard Castle School. His family tree went back to Muker, as does Laurie's. He sent me it, which I thought was very kind of him, when he didn't know me. We are sure now that the connection is Elsie and Ernest. Laurie's mother was cousin to Ernest C. Alderson, who was the policeman's father.

* * * * *

There may be Aldersons, who were well off and who think they are of better stock than their neighbours over the road. But going back a generation or two or three, and they are probably from the same ancestor. No better than each other, they come from the same blood.

Some people are better educated, have more chances, and more help, financially. Ability is something you are born with or not, but whatever education or status people have, it makes them no better. We are all the same. Somebody has a great-great-grandfather landowner. The land always passed to the eldest son. The others could be poor. It would be interesting to know if you are related to royalty or prosperity in the past.

Maybe you are poor now, but have that feeling that you have not always been. Maybe generations ago, your family was well off. It's the luck of the draw. I love to bring people together.

* * * * * *

On 10 July, 2001, I phoned Barnard Castle Boarding School, and spoke to Mrs Blankard, a very helpful lady, to see if there was any information on Ernest, and awaited a promised letter.

* * * * * *

On 7th August I had a letter back from Barnard Castle Board School about the ex-policeman's father. It only gives dates he joined and so on, nothing more than there would be on any other person – nothing that made him different.

John Alderson says his father was good at mathematics. John Alderson says he's good at love. We are all supposed to come from the DNA of just seven women – John says if he comes from the DNA of one of the seven women, he hopes she was a nice one!

Chapter 17

Hannah Hauxwell

This foot and mouth is messing me about. I want to take photographs of the old farms where my families have lived – all those linked to me. I feel more secure, and have a sense of belonging – I'm beginning to get my confidence back. But I don't think the paths will be open to the public this year.

I have started to go down my own path in life, and I will not have anything stop me again! The foot and mouth has me angry. This is forcing me to stop. I haven't the time to stop! I've lost so much time as it is, being ill. I'm frightened to stop! I'm just finding reality, the real world! Or has it all been a dream?

This has really set me back! I can't get near to photograph!

* * * * * *

The grey drystone walling going up and
Down with the curvature of the lay of the land,
It also marks out each farm's boundary.
These walls have stood for hundreds of years
In all weathers in Stainmore.

The lusciously green grassed area of South Stainmore
To the grey stony wind-swept terrain of North Stainmore.

* * * * * *

Sunday 5th August 2001 – I wrote to Hannah Hauxwell twice in the year 2000. I would love to visit her and write a book like the ones about her life, but she didn't write back. One day, I will pay her a visit at Cotherstone, Belle Vue.

We went to take a photograph of Hannah Hauxwell's house, Belle Vue, a white-fronted house next to the pub.

They say it is best to call after 12 o'clock as she gets up late. She is recovering from a broken hip or leg, after she had a fall.

The car broke down on the way to Brough so we had to turn around on the Stainmore road. Don't talk to me about that Stainmore road. The car began to struggle after we left Cotherstone. The car was giving up, and so was I, and what about my photos? We had to push the car up every hill after leaving Staindrop. It gave up on the Coniscliff road. What a nightmare. It was an adventure to Michelle – she thought it was great fun.

* * * * * *

Hannah's home in Cotherstone

On Sunday, 24th August 2003, we travelling back from reservoir, which is where I like to go to get away from it all, to relax. I asked Bob to drive through Cotherstone. I was going to give it one last try to see Hannah Hauxwell.

We went in the pub at Cotherstone, had a drink, and then we went back to sit in the car. I told Bob I would only be five minutes. He said she would never come to the door, but this was because locals say this.

I knocked at the door and I saw a head move inside the window. She looked at me, and I said hello, and asked if she had just one minute to spare. I think she could have gone, but I said it again, and smiled at her – 'One minute, please.'

She seemed to take notice, and went to her side door and opened it. I couldn't believe my luck. It was Hannah in the flesh! I was overwhelmed.

I told her that she doesn't know how much this means to me, to meet her. I think she was wondering what I was so pleased about. She had lovely silver-grey hair, and to me, she could well have been an Angel.

She let me into her front room, and I noticed how much she was the person in the book, quiet, loving and gentle. She made me feel at ease. I told her that my ancestors had also lived at Hury, where she had lived and farmed, and how I loved the land, and researched the people, and really felt a true passion for the way of life and the values that these people had. I mentioned names like Wilfred Robson, Laurie's brother. He had farmed at Brisco, Baldersdale, for about thirty years. She knew him, and other people I mentioned.

She smiled, and seemed to be at ease with me. I told her I was an Alderson, a Cleasby by marriage. She had known people of both names. I told her I was hoping to write a book about the area, and would mention her in it. I asked if I could shake her hand, and I gave her a kiss on her cheek. She wondered what was so special about her, but I told her she was a really special lady to me. I had been given the opportunity to meet her. I was really grateful. I bid her goodbye, and went on my way. When I got back into the car, I told Bob that I had met her. It was wonderful, like a dream. I was on a high for the rest of the day. Dreams do come true if you wait and be patient.

Chapter 18

Eerie feelings at Stainmore

When looking for Dowgill for research on the Watsons, we passed Pennistone Green. We did not go looking for it, as it was not named on our map, but it seemed to want us to see it – it found us. It was near a chapel.

    I remembered that Laurie had once said that he and his ancestors had lived there. On this day out, we walked about and took photographs. My brother Barrie, who was with us at the time, was more interested in the house opposite, because the old patched-up caravan outside it was full of bullet holes.

    'Look at that!' he said.

    We all felt a little unsafe, but there was not a person in sight.

    After taking a photo of Dowgill from a distance, because of the foot and mouth, we crossed behind the Punch Bowl, which is a big pub on the A66, to the other side of North Stainmore. I wanted to get a picture of Dummah Hill, where in 1827, William Cleasby and Esther née Smith had lived for a short time, but because of the foot and mouth we could not get up the track we wanted to. It had a notice on it – Keep Out.

    We went as far as Borrowdale House and saw what must have been fifty moles hung up by their heads on barbed wire, rotting and swaying in the wind. It was horrible, very disturbing to me, since I'd never lived on a farm. It made me feel sick. I had perhaps had a romantic idea of country life before. Was this the reality? I felt as though farmers were only butchers.

    I said to Bob, 'Let's get away from them. Why do farmers do that?'

    So we reversed down the lane and, to my horror, there was a dead stiff cat with all four legs stuck out up into the air.

    'Look at that, Bob! It's horrible! Let's get out of here. It's creepy!' I think I could sense that something was wrong, or had happened there. This place was telling me something. I think all my senses were working overtime on that day out. I couldn't get home quick enough. The fear was intense inside me. I was not well when we'd set out for the journey, and now I had a mixture of a migraine headache, of being not a very good traveller in any case, and of being on medication. The tension of my research was getting to me. I think now that I was most likely running away from my fear of reality. Do I show my character well!

Chapter 19

Phone call with Glennis

On Friday 4 October, I phoned Glennis, Laurie's friend, and told her that I was going to take back the directory that I had of Laurie's. This was a local directory of Stainmore from 1900 which listed names and addresses of farms in the area.

She said that Laurie was out visiting his sister, Violet, who was ill, and taking a present round to his granddaughter. It was her birthday, and she was 18 years old.

The death of Laurie's only son and his first born had been a great loss. Pennistone Green was Laurie's home and had been home to the Cleasbys for many generations. It seemed like something had drawn me to Pennistone Green. It had been the home of Isobella Watson's (née Robson) family, great-great-uncle Joseph George Watson's wife.

Laurie had and still has great love for his son. If his son was anything like Laurie, he would have been a wonderful person, I'm sure. This is why Laurie had been so proud of him. Laurie is such a lovely man, kind and helpful. I'm sure I was meant to find him. Maybe he was in need of a friend. He had lost a son and gained a friend.

In October Bob has a day's holiday, so we went to take the directory back to Laurie at Penrith. I got as far as Brough and was very sick. I asked Bob to go on to Penrith with the directory. It was raining very heavily. I stayed at Brough, and had a walk about. I went to get cups of tea to feel better. Then I saw Glennis. She had come with Laurie on hearing I was ill. Bob had gone on to Orton to get a photo of Low Moor, but I'm not sure if he got it. We all met in the flower shop, Brough. I bought a wooden cross. So did Glennis. Laurie took Glennis home to Darlington. It was really nice to see them.

* * * * * *

Bob and I went on to Bowes. We took a photo of Sleightholme in the distance because of foot and mouth, also maybe Mellwaters – there was so much haziness, and the weather was so bad, we could hardly be sure. Those sheep over there are very afraid of people. Went to look in Bowes churchyard, but we didn't see any Cleasby headstones.

Chapter 20

He was trying to scare us (The Missing Link)

When Grandad was ill after a stroke, he once revealed to my mother that she was brave having married into the family, as it was related to Mary Ann Cotton. This scandal happened in the 60s. His wife, my dad's mam, Ursula Alderson, was in hospital for many years suffering from depression. She died in hospital.

Nothing was said about this until I began my family research. I knew that on the old 1962 will there was the name of Laurie Robson of Stainmore, so I thought that this would have been the family Grandad was referring to, as Mary Ann's maiden name was Robson.

I looked very deeply into this theory, asking people if they knew anything, but nobody had ever heard about a link to her.

At first, I thought they were being not very helpful. I was getting nowhere! But I eventually realized that I had got it wrong. I needed to look elsewhere in my research to find it.

I bought a book on Mary Ann's life, and came across the fact that her mother's maiden name was Lonsdale. I needed to find the name somewhere in my findings. I had never come across it before, but there were some of the children from the marriage of Thomas Alderson of Newfield and Ellen Peart that I had not accounted for.

I eventually found the marriage of Sarah Ann Alderson and Robert Lonsdale at Binchester Cottages, Primitive Methodist Chapel in Auckland, on 11 September 1907. They both lived at Newfield.

I now had a lead on the name 'Lonsdale', and had found that the connection was the family of Thomas of Newfield.

I put an article in a local newspaper asking for anybody who knew the descendants of the family. I also looked at the census return for Newfield and found that Robert Lonsdale's father, William Lonsdale, was born at West Rainton. He was a miner.

I then looked in my book on Mary Ann's life and it said that her mother's father had mined and lived at East, and West Rainton, for many years at Hazard Pit. Were these people from the same family? This was a theory, but it needed to be confirmed by somebody else, who knew it to be true. It turned out that they were.

The day came when I received a reply to my newspaper appeal from one of the grandchildren of Sarah Ann Alderson's brother, Joseph Alderson. She got in touch with me from Dorset. Her name was Maureen Morton, née Alderson. She confirmed details about our family connections. We were related to each other.

She told me that the Lonsdale family had moved to Chilton after getting married in Newfield, and that they had no children, only an adopted son.

I told her about Grandad's story of Mary Cotton. Maureen was quiet for quite a few seconds, and then said she had heard it also, but only because she had big ears as a child – it was never told to her.

Since we'd both heard it, this was verification that what we'd heard was right. At last the mystery was over for my parents. I had solved the muddle, and I now know that Grandad always told the truth. It was hard work for me finding something from nothing again, but this is what I like to do.

Mary Ann Cotton was hanged for murder on 24 March 1873, in Durham Gaol. She had poisoned her family with arsenic. The descendants I had found were from the brother of Mary Ann's mother, called Lonsdale.

I had also found that Thomas Alderson of Newfield started up the Temperance Hall there, which became the working men's club without any alcohol. It was somewhere for the miners to go during their short leisure hours without returning home drunk and causing trouble for their families. Thomas died in Newfield in 1937 at the age of 87 years.

* * * * * *

While I was finding out about Mary Ann Cotton, it was very frightening to me, since she hurt people. I was only looking for good things that supported me, not things that depressed me, and made me feel bad. People hurt me. I only wanted to find good people.

I read the book about her in the library, and it made me feel uneasy. Maybe that is why things like this are best left forgotten. It affects people's minds. To me it was like a bad nightmare, and I had a few of those when I was ill.

I think at the time there was stigma attached to the family connected with her, and to anyone marrying into the family. It is not something to boast about! You keep quiet, keep it a secret!

But then there is Thomas Alderson of Newfield. What a good man he sounds. I think I've found one to be proud of here. I would like to be like him. He sounds strong and fair, and cares about people.

Chapter 21

Tuesday 6 November
Finding out about Startforth and Bowes, Cleasbys and Johnsons:
Where Esther Cleasby lived (1861)

I phoned Startforth Primary School and they thought a Mr Tony Liverseed from Startforth might be able to help me.

He told me that there was an index of people who were buried in Startforth Churchyard. There used to be a pub in Startforth, which is not there now, called the George IV. He said it might have been the beer house that John Johnson, a cousin of the Cleasbys, had owned in 1861. William Cleasby had died, aged 42 years, and his wife, Esther Cleasby née Smith, and the children, lived with John Johnson's family. Esther worked at the beer house as a char.

Mr Liverseed said he once knew a June Cleasby, who worked at Glaxo, Barnard Castle. He said he would ask around about her, and took my phone number. He got back to me with the phone number of June Cleasby. She had lived at Bowes for most of her life, but when I rang her she could only tell me about her own family.

I needed more certificates. I needed to search St Catherine's House Registers in the reference library or archives.

First, I tried to find the record of the death of Esther Cleasby née Smith. I looked over a twenty year span, but not one entry could be found. My next thought was that she must have married again, and in that way changed her name. I then had to look for marriages and found one for an Esther Cleasby, which took place in the Teesdale area on 18 May 1864.

I sent away for the certificate. It gave details of her father, Thomas Smith, and that she had married a 58-year-old widower, called Charles Hutchinson. He was from Barnard Castle, and she lived at Bowes.

Esther's youngest son, James Cleasby, who was my husband's great grandfather, came to Thornaby, which is close to Middlesbrough, where we now live.

I traced his marriage certificate. He married Elizabeth Cliff at Stockton Register Office on 26 October 1869. James lived at William Street, Thornaby, and was 25 years old when he married, but to my surprise, he was listed as a widower.

Now I needed to find out when he first married. I needed to search the indexes again, and found recorded James' first marriage to Mary Nevison on 7 July 1866, when James was 21 years old. His profession was labourer in the iron works.

Next, I traced the death certificate of his father, William Cleasby, and on receiving it, found that he had died of asthma and dropsy on 24 November 1842, at Bowes. My husband, Thomas Robert Cleasby, also has asthma, so maybe it is hereditary.

I next found out that Charles Hutchinson and his wife Esther lived at Barnard Castle in 1971, at Burton's Yard. He was 65 years old at the time, and his

Private Houses, Eggleston Abbey

occupation was listed as 'driver of omnibus'. Esther was still alive, aged 64, with no stated occupation.

As a matter of interest to me, I noticed that the Darlington District Bank Manager at this time of 1871 was a William Dent, Market Place Bank, Barnard Castle. He was one of the Dent family of Hunderthwaite, who keep cropping up in my research, with connections to both the Alderson and Cleasby families, and connections in Thringarth, Romaldkirk and Stainmore. It's a small world. Families keep coming back together. I would just like to say at this point that my grandfather Alderson and Bob's Uncle Herbert Cleasby worked together at the ICI Billingham Ammonia Works when Grandad was charge hand of the no. 2 urea plant.

I found that Esther Hutchinson died on 23 November 1879 at the Market Place, Barnard Castle, aged 72 years. Her husband, Charles Hutchinson, a cab driver at the time, was the informant of the death.

Then another spot of luck – I found that Mary Ann Cleasby and Matthew Maynell married on 19 May 1860. They both lived at Barnard Castle, Mary Ann being the daughter of Esther Cleasby, who married Charles Hutchinson. Mary Ann's father was William Cleasby, deceased of Bowes.

After a lengthy search of many years, I finally traced the death of Esther's mother-in-law, Dorothy Cleasby, who died on 17 November 1864, aged 93 years. Her residence at the time of her death was Eggleston Abbey. Her late husband was William Cleasby, who had been a butcher.

I got in touch with district probate to see if Dorothy Cleasby might have left her home to her family, but there was not a copy of grant or will to an estate from the beginning of 1864 through to 1867, the time after Dorothy's death.

The 1851 census for Eggleston Abbey shows a Dorothy Cleasby as being 80 years old, and says she was born in Wensleydale. It also shows the family of Ann Elliot, 41 years old and born at Bowes. Ann Elliot is named on Dorothy's death certificate as informant.

A William Cleasby lived at Cragg House, Stainmore, in 1829. This is likely to be Esther's husband. He later died at Bowes. When he married Esther from Stainmore, the family lived near Esther's parents on Stainmore.

* * * * * *

In April 2002, I found out where Bog House, Bowes, had stood. Mr Liverseed helped me again. He got me a contact with the family from Bar Gap. The ruins of Bog House were opposite to the Sleightholme Farm, which is today on the Pennine Way. William Cleasby was born at Bog House, Bowes, in 1799. His parents were William Cleasby, a butcher, and Dorothy Cleasby, née Webster.

I received the 1861 census on 1 May, which shows Dorothy Cleasby aged 90 years living with her daughter, Ann Elliot, born in Sleightholme, aged 50 years, and Ann's husband Thomas, at Private House, Eggleston Abbey. There is a Cleasby Hill south-east of Sleightholme Farm in Arkengarthdale, in the original county of

Sleightholme Farm, Bowes

The site of Bog House, Bowes. The original stones have been used for an enclosure today

The Market Place, Barnard Castle

Cleasby's Yard, The Bank, Barnard Castle

North Yorkshire. We made a trip out to Sleightholme Farm, and took pictures.
    We then walked over to the spot where Bog House had stood. There is a walled enclosure there today. To get to it, you have to cross very boggy land and cross Sleightholme Beck. In winter, the whole area would be very flooded. The house was on a raised area surrounded by boggy land. You would have had to wade across it some two hundred years ago. Bob's ancestors would not have had any wellington boots in those days!
    The area seemed to be the most remote moorland that we have visited in all my research – rabbits and pheasants and very hardy sheep in this very moist and untouched landscape. It is a beautiful scenic area, and very peaceful.
    It is said that Bog House, which was the gamekeeper's house, stood on the same spot in the 1600s. Now, it is only a pile of stones, with a tree growing in the middle of it. There is one wall more intact than the rest at one end, and sheep use this for shelter.
    Another farm of the Cleasbys' was Dry Gill, which is further on from Bog House, but all that is left at the spot is a walled enclosure. It must have been a very hard and desolate place to live some two hundred years ago.
    When we left Bowes and paid a visit to Barnard Castle, we stumbled across a Cleasby's Yard, with its entrance on the Bank, which is the main road through Barnard Castle. The yard was named after the family of Cleasby who lived there.
    In 1894, a Thomas Cleasby was a coachbuilder who lived at the Bank, Barnard Castle. This Thomas Cleasby was married to Ann, née Smith. On the 1891 census, they were both stated as being born at Stainmore. They were married in 1856 at Brough.
    Thomas Cleasby's father was William, and Ann's father was Thomas Smith, who I am sure, was the brother of our Esther Smith.
    With research, I think that in 1829, Thomas Cleasby's father, William Cleasby, lived at Cragg House, Stainmore, and that Ann Smith's father, Thomas Smith, was born in 1829 at Grey's Lodge, Stainmore.
    In 1829, a Robert Cleasby lived at Palliard, Stainmore, and John Cleasby lived at Pennistone Green, and also at Heggerscales and Rookby at later times.
    The origin of the name 'Cleasby' is traced to a place, Cleasby, located in Yorkshire. The name was originally applied to one who was a local of Cleasby Village. It appears to be Scandinavian. The 'by' on the end of 'Cleasby' means 'settlement'.

* * * * *

In 2003 the most interesting information I received was from Hazel Cleasby, née Tarn, of Appleby-in-Westmorland. She, with the help of the Reverend Ingram Cleasby, and my own information, has managed to take the Cleasby family tree back further to a Thomas Cleasby, a Quaker, and Mary of Stowgill, Stainmore. They had a daughter, Frances, and a son, Edward. Edward died in 1716, and had a flock of

270 sheep, a very large flock for those days. He lived at Clove Lodge, Baldersdale, and also lived in West Stonesdale.

We also found that a Robert Cleasby died at Stowgill, Stainmore in 1579. This really takes us back a long way. I love to see how it all fits together.

Chapter 22

Signing the Queen Mother's Book of Condolences at Bowes Museum, Barnard Castle, Sunday 7 April 2002

The Queen Mother died on 30 March 2002. I had always wanted to pay a visit to Bowes Museum with it being in the heart of the community of my own and my husband's ancestral past. I was drawn to go after the Queen Mother died. I felt it was the right time. I knew I had to go and visit the museum, and sign the Book of Condolences.

The museum had been donated by the Queen Mother's ancestors. I was really impressed by the amount of objects on view. It was really splendid – first class. To me, the Queen Mother represented everything that was good, showing warmth and kindness to ordinary people. When she died, it was the end of a special era.

The museum was donated by John Bowes, who had acquired his wealth from his father's ancestors who owned the mines. He had gone to live in France, having married Josephine née Benoite, a French actress. They had no children due to his wife's ill-health, and she died at the age of 48 years in 1874.

John decided to come back to his roots, Barnard Castle, to give something back to the people in the area, in his remembrance. John died in 1885 before the museum was completed in 1892.

I signed the Book of Remembrance for the Queen Mother, whose ancestors were the Bowes-Lyon family.

In my research in past years, I had found that in 1561, Sir George Bowes and John Bowes Esquire had owned the land of Mickleton, Lune and Thringarth Park, which are in the Teesdale area. In 1608, the owners of the land gave the right to the people of Mickleton to clear the forested area so that they could farm the land.

The 1823 directory shows the main landowners to be James Dent, John Dent and Joseph Rain. My ancestors owned land at Thringarth and Romaldkirk around these times.

On looking at a map in the Bowes Museum, Romaldkirk, in 1578, is written as 'Rumbaldkirk'.

The funeral of the Queen Mother took place at Westminster Abbey on 9 April. I watched it on the television. She was then laid to rest at Windsor next to her beloved husband, Bertie, King George VI.

As well as going to Bowes, we also visited Eggleston Abbey, which was the last home of my husband's great-great-great-grandmother, Dorothy Cleasby, who lived at Bowes for most of her life.

This day out was lovely, as we did not break down like we had on our last trip. We had to get a new car after the last trip, so our visit was a smooth one.

Bowes Museum, signing the Queen Mother's book of rememberance

Bowes Museum

Chapter 23

Returning to the present

I feel I have come to the end of my journey to the past. I think it is time to live life now. The journey was a hard but joyful one, a way of replacing one bad depression with a hard task, with the same feelings of pressure. I used the pressure I was under to drive me on.

The dark clouds are lifting now. I desire to be the person I used to be, and place myself back in the present moment, and see what the future has to offer me. The one thing I do now know, is that I have firm roots, stronger than I ever knew before. Maybe it was something I needed to find out about myself, when I felt lost and out of control.

I had no control over my research – it was something drawing me on, despite myself. Writing it down helped me to communicate it to the real world. I felt I had been sucked through a tunnel and spat out at the other end, that I was in some play. I really needed to write it down, my experiences and thoughts, and put it into a book, so that I can put the book on to the shelf where it belongs, and finalise the whole episode.

I didn't know what I was heading for, but it was peace of mind. I have come out, alive, at the other end. This world is a lovely place to live in, and knowledge of the past is a good thing to have.

Not only have I found my family through my research, but I have also found friends. I have met people from the wider community, all those who have helped me, with directions or local knowledge.

There is a lovely lady called Judy, who works in a flower shop and café in Brough, where Joseph George Watson, my great-grandfather's half-brother died.

Every time we go there, we visit her, often meeting Laurie and Glennis in the café, which is a meeting-place for many of the local people. Judy is very friendly, and welcomes us each time.

She has known Laurie for a long time, and she had also lived, in the 50s, at Greena, where my great-great-grandmother lived. This is how she would have first met Laurie, who also lived near Greena. It's a small world when you start researching in rural areas.

I wonder what the rest of my life has to offer, or if I can help someone else with their life? People need to find themselves, they need to look deep within, and be honest and kind to themselves. They need to listen to what their needs are. I followed my heart and instincts to get me through a really hard time.

But I got there. Other people do things differently. Maybe I do things the hard way. I have always been a hard worker. I've turned my life around. I found what I was looking for, the real me, my roots and all.

Tough times never last, but tough people do...

Michelle my niece

At the end of my work

Family trees are strong

The roots go down deep

I drew strength

from my roots.

They feed me.

Acknowledgements

To especially my husband, Bob Cleasby, who chauffered me around and supported me throughout. Mr Laurie Robson, a Stainmore man, for being such a good friend and helper over the last ten years, and also Glennis. Mrs Christine Hennes, my long-lost relative from Saskatchewan, Canada. Mrs Maxine Payne, Middleton-in-Teesdale, and Maureen Morton née Alderson, Portland, Dorset.

    Also to many good friends who have supported and helped me along the way including: my doctor, neighbours Brian and Hazel Davison, and Val. Linda Evans and Kath from Brambles Foods, not forgetting Peter, who was fun to work with. My cousin Jean, who always gave me encouragement to write my book, even though I was sometimes very ill. My cousin Joan, for reading and typing my notes. Many thanks to all of my family, that I can be part of their lives. A special thank you to my father. Also to the Alderson Family History Society for having me as a member and to everyone else who has helped.

Life's been a bit of a battle, but I'm still sailing through. So can you. We all need to be inspired by something, but you have to search to find it. This is who I am now and that is where I came from.

Wendy Cleasby, 2003

The last word

Wendy and I were both born and bred on Teesside; I was very fortunate to meet Wendy 20 years ago, and consider myself very lucky to have done so.

She has been a faithful friend and soul mate and is a loving and caring wife, who has put one hundred percent effort into writing her first book. It is about the ups and downs of her life, and her family and friends, both present and past.

I am delighted that she has been able to regain her self-confidence and that she has found her way back to living a happy and normal life where she belongs.

Wendy's loving husband, Bob